OVERCOM SELECTIVE MUTISM

The Parent's Field Guide

Aimee Kotrba, PhD & Shari J. Saffer

Published by
Summit & Krest Publishing
Charleston, SC 29464

Printed in the United States of America

ISBN: 978-1-7325996-0-4

ACKNOWLEDGEMENTS

A big thank-you to Connie Kotrba, Alison Siroky M.S., Jenny Foster, Katelyn Reed M.S. and Anne Andrus for editing and giving thoughtful feedback on this book despite your busy schedules. To the rest of our family and friends who so generously provided support, thank you!

Aimee Kotrba, Ph.D

Many people say it, but I truly mean it – I have the best family and support system. To Jeff – you make every day better, and you give me the room and encouragement to be fully me. I love you always. To Baylee, Morgan, and Isaac – I don't think I really knew what fun was (or what the word tired truly meant!) until I had you. You three make my days and my dreams brighter than before. Finally, my heartfelt appreciation to those who work with me at Thriving Minds Behavioral Health for your support and for sharing in my excitement. I am so blessed to work with all of you.

Shari J. Saffer

Anna, you are amazing, more courageous than you know and more loved than you can imagine. The sky is the limit for you. Emilie, you might rule the world one day. When you do, please remember your mom who loves you dearly. Andrew, you are the rock of our family and I can't imagine taking this journey without you. Your love of family and sacrifice do not go unnoticed - we love you. To the rest of my family, friends and community - I have reached that phase in life where "I can see clearly now" and I don't know how I got so lucky to have so many extraordinary people in my corner. It is because of you that we have come so far. You know who you are, and I hope you know how much you mean to us.

Our cover imagery is meant to convey a motivating and meaningful experience. The *labyrinth*, as shown in the foreground, is thought to be an ancient symbol of a meandering but purposeful path, representing personal transformation. Evidence suggests that labyrinths date back hundreds of years - they have been used for meditation, healing and even to represent a pilgrimage for religious purposes. While the history is not always clear, it is believed by some that a labyrinth can represent the journey to our inner core and back out again into the world. Life is about the journey - not the destination…

"Your life is a sacred journey. And it is about change, growth, discovery, movement, transformation, continuously expanding your vision of what is possible, stretching your soul, learning to see clearly and deeply, listening to your intuition, taking courageous challenges at every step along the way. You are on the path... exactly where you are meant to be right now... And from here, you can only go forward, shaping your life story into a magnificent tale of triumph, of healing, of courage, of beauty, of wisdom, of power, of dignity, and of love." **–Caroline Adams**

Please be kind to yourself and know that you (and your child) will get where you need to be. Move forward in your time…

Shari & Aimee

CONTENTS

Dear Reader,

A few years ago, I wrote a book on selective mutism (SM) entitled *Selective Mutism: An Assessment and Intervention Guide for Therapists, Educators, and Parents*. My intent was to shed light on the effective interventions for SM, and how to create those opportunities to practice being brave in the therapy office, classroom, and beyond. This book provided information on how SM develops and how to assess for it and laid the groundwork for understanding the behavioral intervention strongly recommended by research. However, I realize that many parents could benefit from additional support in order to navigate the path toward successful intervention for their children with SM – it can be a confusing, time-consuming, and lonely road. In order to support parents and provide more hands-on guidance through that process, I teamed up with Shari Saffer, a mother of a child with selective mutism. Together, we have written this book as an informational guide, workbook, and handout manual for parents, and we hope that it is also helpful for teachers, therapists, caregivers, and any others who know, love, and want to do the very best to help a child with SM.

–Aimee Kotrba, Ph.D.

Chapter One

WHY DOESN'T MY CHILD SPEAK?

The journey begins for many parents with an appointment at a psychologist's office after their son's (or daughter's) teacher or a school representative has contacted them. The bewildered parent reports their seemingly normal child is not speaking outside of the home. The parents are confused – he speaks easily at home; and although he is considered "shy" by family members, he does have friends in the neighborhood with whom he talks and plays. However, his teacher and school staff are reporting that he is silent and appears frozen in normal school settings. He makes poor eye contact and rarely engages other children in play during recess. His parents are understandably upset and wonder: If he speaks at home, why isn't he speaking at school? Perhaps he is trying to get out of doing schoolwork? Maybe he simply doesn't like his teacher? Could he have been bullied on the playground?

Confusion, frustration, and helplessness are among the ways peers and adults may react to a child with SM, a child who may exhibit physical freezing, poor eye contact, and difficulty responding to and initiating verbal communication. The key component of selective mutism is a fear of speaking in situations outside of the home. Many children with SM struggle to speak with peers and adults in school and in public, as well as with extended family or family friends. Selective mutism is relatively rare and is estimated to occur in only 1% of the population which makes it difficult for parents and school personnel to recognize it.

- ☀ **Common traits of SM include**: difficulty initiating communication or responding verbally and nonverbally, poor eye contact, physical freezing, delay in responding (long pause between the question and the child's response), slowness to "warm up" to people, anxiety around engaging in social interactions (especially group social situations such as birthday parties or in less structured social interactions such as recess)

- ☀ **Other challenges for children with SM can include:** generalized anxiety, specific phobias, toileting issues, sensory issues, language disorders or interrupted speech fluency, obsessive-compulsive traits, separation anxiety, social anxiety (including eating in front of others, speaking or performing in front of a group, asking to use the bathroom), cognitive inflexibility, and fears about using the public restroom

Due to the lack of public knowledge about SM and the typical nature of children with selective mutism (generally quiet, unassuming, well-behaved, likeable, and academically competent), many children do not receive an official diagnosis or begin treatment until approximately 6-9 years of age. However, historical reports by parents suggest that symptoms of SM begin much earlier – around 2-4 years of age. Typically, children with SM exhibit anxiety or hesitancy in social speaking from a very early age, but it is not recognized as a "problem" until the child enters school. The child may be completely silent in preschool or may speak to a few peers or adults in the preschool setting, but upon entry to elementary school many children regress or have increasing difficulty in speaking (perhaps due to increased academic and performance demands, a longer school day, or more children in the environment).

Many children with SM are also socially reluctant or have social anxiety. Social anxiety and SM frequently go together and have overlapping characteristics; however, they are currently considered two distinct diagnoses. Social anxiety is defined as a fear of social evaluation and judgement. This discomfort can lead to physical symptoms including sweating, headaches, stomachaches, and a rapid heartrate. The outcome of this discomfort or anxiety is typically avoidance of social situations. In contrast, SM is best conceptualized as a specific phobia – a specific fear of speaking or communicating. However, children with SM may or may not describe it is a "fear;" instead, they more commonly describe it as a difficulty or discomfort, or even a lack of desire/motivation to speak in social situations. Approximately 90% of children diagnosed with SM will also experience the symptoms of social anxiety. Clinical experience and research (Oerbeck, Overgaard, Stein, Pripp, & Kristensen, 2018) suggest that those 10% of children who do not have co-existing social anxiety are easier to treat and respond faster to treatment. They may also have better long-term outcomes because they do not experience the "double anxiety" of worrying about others hearing their voice and possibly judging or evaluating them.

Currently, prevalence rates suggest that girls are twice as likely to receive a diagnosis of SM in comparison to their male counterparts (Dummit, et al., 1997). We are not entirely certain why this phenomenon occurs; some hypotheses include:

- **Hypothesis 1** – Women are more likely to struggle with anxiety disorders at any age.
- **Hypothesis 2** – There is a social expectation that girls will be more talkative and socially engaging, and when a girl does not meet these social standards it is more apparent/striking, therefore leading to evaluation and diagnosis.
- **Hypothesis 3** – Boys who exhibit these same characteristics may be incorrectly diagnosed with Autism Spectrum Disorder or Oppositional Defiant Disorder

There is a lot of misinformation about the development of selective mutism. Some laypeople (and even professionals!) still believe that lack of speech is secondary to a trauma in the child's history. Some misinterpret it as oppositionality, defiance, or willfulness. However, research leans toward anxiety that has been increased by environmental, biological, genetic, and temperamental factors.

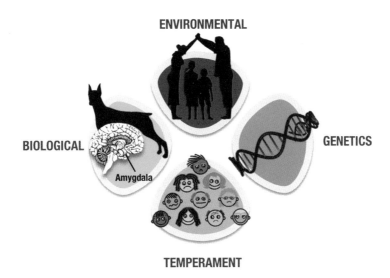

Selective mutism develops through several factors, but the focus of most research is on the pattern of learned avoidance of speaking. Children with SM may be born with a genetic predisposition for anxiety, and therefore when they are placed in situations with any possible social or performance component, their overactive amygdala (the brain's guard dog) screams "Danger!" and sets into motion the fight, flight, or freeze response. Our amygdala exists to keep us safe, and when it perceives any danger it prepares our body to respond in a way that will keep us safe and alive. It sends more oxygen to the blood or muscles to help them run, fight, or hold still. It tenses the muscles so that they can spring into action. It quickens the heartrate to push blood to large muscles. It allows for faster thinking and racing thoughts. It even slows down "unnecessary" bodily actions, like digestion, to focus on keeping the body safe (this, coupled with tensed stomach muscles, can explain why stomachaches can occur with anxiety). Our body is an amazing and efficient protector….except that in this scenario, no one needs protection! Our body makes us believe that we are in *danger* when we are only in *discomfort*!

When children enter social situations (e.g., school, playdates, extracurricular activities, etc.) with an overactive amygdala, they use the typical human coping response to anxiety – avoidance! They try to exit the situation, have parents/peers/siblings/adults speak for them, freeze and don't respond, or give a fearful or even defiant look to the person trying to engage them. Most adults and peers can feel the child's anxiety and hesitancy to respond, and they do not want to push the child or make them uncomfortable; others step in and "rescue" by responding for the child, reducing or completely extinguishing questions or prompts to speak, or only asking questions that can be responded to nonverbally (i.e., nodding, pointing, writing, etc.).

> Just like we might choose a different hiking path if we know a bear was spotted on a trail up ahead, children who are anxious have a tendency to stay away from what causes their body to shout, 'Danger'.

Our kind attempts at ***rescuing*** the child from their anxiety only serve to ***reinforce*** the child's anxiety. Rescuing may make them feel better in the short-term (it feels good to escape from things that make us nervous or uncomfortable), but it accidentally suggests to the child that they cannot or should not handle the discomfort that comes with responding. Worst of all, we all practice this cycle of behavior numerous times per day, hundreds of times per week, thousands of times per year! The child becomes quite good at *avoiding* and the people around the child become quite good at *rescuing*! Thus, the older the child, the harder it is to break this cycle (and treat selective mutism) because everyone has become exceedingly good at their role.

Reducing "rescuing" behavior is an important step in helping your child be brave, and in Chapter 5 we will discuss behavioral intervention, including how to reduce accidental rescuing. At this point, simply increasing your awareness of rescuing should help you to begin thinking about the ways in which you might help to break the cycle.

Selective Mutism Subtypes

Recent research suggests that there may be three subtypes of selective mutism (Mulligan & Shipon-Blum, 2015). While understanding the subtypes can be helpful in planning an individual child's treatment or intervention, each child is different and some children with SM may not fit neatly into one of these categories.

SM Subtype	Key Behavioral Indicators	Intervention/Treatment Impacts
Anxious		
<ul><li>May exhibit overt anxiety</li><li>Might freeze & avoid eye contact</li><li>May use passive avoidance (freeze or flight response)</li></ul>	<ul><li>Request that parents speak for them</li><li>May look down when spoken to</li><li>May focus on nonverbal communicative behaviors</li></ul>	<ul><li>Generally more compliant with intervention and more easily responsive to treatment</li><li>May require less external motivators (prizes)</li><li>Best engaged using a stepwise intervention and verbal encouragement</li></ul>
Anxious-Oppositional		
<ul><li>Might appear defiant or sassy when prompted to speak</li><li>May use active avoidance (fight response)</li></ul>	<ul><li>May run from the situation</li><li>Might give dirty looks</li><li>Could hit parents when they do not speak for the child</li><li>Make statements such as, "I will not speak to that person!"</li><li>Do not appear to be willingly compliant with treatment goals</li></ul>	<ul><li>Generally need more external motivators (prizes and privileges linked to brave work)</li><li>Parents often need to spend time and effort practicing and perfecting compliance with their child</li><li>Child may need boundary setting and structure to comply</li></ul>

SM Subtype	Key Behavioral Indicators	Intervention/Treatment Impacts
Anxious-Communication Delayed		
☀ May use passive or active avoidance ☀ Clear evidence of a language delay or disorder ☀ Language abilities appear to impact the development and/or maintenance of the mutism	☀ Might exhibit any of the behavioral indicators above	☀ Speech/language therapy to improve speech should occur alongside SM brave work; the quality of speech improves as does the child's confidence in producing speech ☀ Intervention team will usually include a speech pathologist focused on improving/speech/articulation/fluency/word finding ☀ The adult should be prepared if the child receives feedback perceived as negative such as, "You sound strange." or "I can't understand you."

Understanding the Myths About SM

Selective mutism is a commonly misunderstood disorder, and this can lead to frustration for parents, schools, and even friends of children with SM. Some common myths about SM include:

Myth: A child with SM is just defiant, and others should demand that they speak.
Truth: Children with SM can at times appear defiant, but research suggests that their lack of speech is driven by anxiety. For example, if you were fearful of spiders and someone asked you to face that fear (hold a big tarantula) you would likely start by politely declining. If that person was pushy and forceful, and demanded that you hold the spider, eventually you would appear defiant – maybe even yelling, crying, or running away! Children with SM may appear oppositional, but their behavior is more likely a nonverbal coping strategy to avoid what they are afraid of – speaking. When faced with a fearful situation, they are unable to politely refuse or use words to express their discomfort.

Myth: Children with SM have a history of abuse, neglect, or trauma that has caused them to stop speaking.
Truth: There is <u>NO</u> evidence of a causal relationship between abuse, neglect, or trauma and the development of selective mutism. In fact, most parents will state that their child showed characteristics of inhibition, fearfulness, anxiety, separation issues, sensitivity, difficulties being soothed, and weaknesses in emotional control from a very young age. This does not indicate that children with SM *cannot* have trauma in their background, but research has not found a direct connection between trauma and the occurrence of SM.

Myth: These children are autistic, not selectively mute.
Truth: Selective mutism and autism spectrum disorder can occur together in the same child, but are distinctly different diagnoses. Selective mutism is a fear of speaking that generally occurs in social or performance situations, but most children speak normally at home and/or when they are comfortable. They may have some social skill weaknesses (due to a

lack of social experiences) but they still understand the perspectives and feelings of others. Kids with SM have a desire to make friends and have relationships.

There are children who qualify both for a diagnosis of SM and ASD; these children tend to present with reduced or no speech in social or performance settings, but more frequent/comfortable speech at home (even if it includes poor pragmatic speech or immature social interactions). They tend to be rigid and have a hard time understanding social dynamics and social reciprocity (back and forth conversations and interactions) even when comfortable. They frequently show restricted and repetitive interests and behaviors. Even when comfortable and verbal, their social interactions may look awkward or immature.

Myth: Adults should simply stop requesting speech or asking the child to engage with them. Eventually, when the child is ready, they will naturally start speaking.
Truth: If we take away all prompts to speak or engage, and don't encourage the child to face their fear, they typically will NOT magically wake up one day ready to talk! It is important that we don't push a child beyond their capacity or ask them to do brave work that is much beyond their current ability, but intervention must include prompting and encouraging a child to move out of their comfort zone and in the direction of being brave and using their voice.

Myth: If people ask the child to do things that are challenging, we will make their anxiety worse and they will shatter.
Truth: Children are tough and resilient. If only we could all possess the capacity for rebounding like children do! It is our job as interventionists to pace the demands carefully, never asking them to do anything they cannot do, but making a child slightly uncomfortable or placing them a little outside of their comfort zone is truly the only way they will grow. What if we only ask a child to read books that are well within their reading level? Only ask them to practice sports at their current level of skill? Only give them lessons on math that they already know? They would never learn more and develop more.

Myth: Children will grow out of SM.
Truth: Many children impacted by SM will NOT just naturally begin to talk. Sometimes well-intentioned school professionals, individuals in the medical community, and even friends and relatives perpetuate this myth. It is incredibly common that families do not show up for treatment for months or even years after first noticing signs and symptoms of SM because others told them that the child would likely grow out of it. Instead, time will pass, the child will practice avoidance of speech, and parents/friends/teachers will accommodate this avoidance and will stop prompting them to speak altogether (in fact, they may even reinforce the avoidance by encouraging the use of gestures, answering by writing or with white boards, using sign language, etc.). This avoidance will become part of the child's behavioral repertoire and will be increasingly difficult to treat. Rather than improving over time, a child's SM symptoms could get worse without intervention.

Instead of "rolling the dice" and waiting to determine if the child will "grow out of it," we encourage families to seek intervention early and fully engage in the intervention. The intervention ideas described in this manual should not be harmful to any child, and can be experienced as fun and reinforcing!

Myth: Parents of children with SM are dysfunctional, hovering, helicopter parents.

Truth: Parents of children with SM tend to be typical, loving parents with one commonality – they have children who are very anxious! Additionally, it is possible that they are anxious themselves, since anxiety has a genetic component and tends to run in families. When somewhat anxious parents see their children become anxious or struggle, they may react by trying to protect them or shield them from discomfort. This is a natural response, especially for parents who know first-hand what anxiety feels like. Before it was widely recognized as an anxiety disorder, it was believed that family dysfunction, abuse, and/or parental pathology contributed to or caused SM. However, we now know that the parents of children with SM employ a wide range of healthy parenting styles and that their families come in all shapes and sizes.

Myth: Selective mutism is difficult to treat.

Truth: A growing body of research suggests that behavioral interventions can be very effective in treating children with selective mutism, with significant outcomes of increased speech and decreased feelings of anxiety. Despite these findings, many psychologists and mental health professionals still believe that SM is difficult to treat, and therefore do not learn intervention strategies or work with children with selective mutism. They are truly missing out. Working effectively with children with SM can be one of the most rewarding professional experiences.

Furthermore, medication has been shown to have positive impacts on reductions in anxiety and increases in the ability to approach uncomfortable situations. Many parents find that children who were unable to fully engage in treatment prior to medication can participate more fully after medication, thereby speeding up intervention time and allowing the child to feel the natural reward of speaking and socially engaging with others. Medications such as Zoloft and Prozac have the most research backing usage for the treatment of selective mutism (Bartarian, et al., 2018). We provide a more detailed discussion on medication in Chapter 5.

Read, Ask, and Learn More About SM

More facts, research, and data on SM can be found in *Selective Mutism: An Assessment and Intervention Guide for Therapists, Educators, and Professionals*. Our intent for this parent guide is to provide just the right amount of background information and knowledge to guide parents so you can directly help your child with SM. We also encourage you to find a good therapist who can help you to help your child (we will discuss how to do this in Chapter 4), but we understand that there are far too few experts in selective mutism. With this is mind, we aim to guide parents to be the incredible change agents we know that you can be!

While you are the expert on your child, beginning the process of supporting a child with SM can be difficult to face alone. You will also benefit from learning more about selective mutism, and from connecting with families who understand your struggle and can congratulate you on your victories. Organizations, books, and social media groups specific to SM can help you to form these connections. Here are some of our favorites:

Books

- *Treatment for Children with Selective Mutism: An Integrated Behavioral Approach*, by R. Lindsey Bergman
- *Lola's/Leo's Words Disappeared*, by Elaheh Bos
- *Maya's Voice*, by Wen-Wen Cheng
- *Helping Children with Selective Mutism and Their Parents: A Guide for School-Based Professionals*, by Christopher Kearney
- *The Selective Mutism Resource Manual, 2nd Edition*, by Alison Wintgens and Maggie Johnson
- *Selective Mutism: An Assessment and Intervention Guide for Therapists, Educators, and Therapists*, by Aimee Kotrba
- *Helping Your Child with Selective Mutism: Practical Steps to Overcome a Fear of Speaking*, by Angela McHolm
- *Charli's Choices*, by Marian Molden
- *The Selective Mutism Treatment Guide: Manuals for Parents, Teachers, and Therapists: Still Waters Run Deep*, by Ruth Peredik
- *Understanding Katie*, by Elisa Shipon-Blum
- *Can I Tell You About Selective Mutism: A Guide for Friends, Family, and Professionals*, by Alison Wintgens and Maggie Johnson

Organizations and Websites

- The Selective Mutism Association: *http://www.selectivemutism.org/*
- Child Mind Institute Webinar Trainings: *https://childmind.org/parent-educator-workshops-selective-mutism/*
- Anxiety BC: *http://www.anxietybc.com/parenting/selective-mutism*
- Selective Mutism Information and Research Association (SMIRA – UK based): *http://www.selectivemutism.org.uk/*
- Selective Mutism Learning University: *http://selectivemutismlearning.org/*

Facebook Social Media Groups

- Parents of Children with Selective Mutism (US based but with active international followers)
- Parents and Caretakers of Teens and Younger Adults with Selective Mutism (US based)
- SMIRA – Selective Mutism Information and Research Association (UK based but with active international followers)
- Selective Mutism Awareness (US based but with international followers)

Seeking out information from these books, websites, and organizations should give you a much clearer picture of what selective mutism is and what it is not. After reading, researching, and learning about SM from different resources, consider again your child's strengths and weaknesses. Do they seem to fit the diagnostic criteria for selective mutism?

Selective Mutism Diagnostic Criteria

* Reluctance or unwillingness to speak to peers in school and in extracurricular or social activities
* Reluctance or unwillingness to speak to adults in school or social activities
* This reluctance is more than "typical" hesitation with strangers or in the first moments of meeting a new person
* This reluctance is maintained past the first month of school
* Normal speech at home or when in comfortable settings (e.g., when no one else is paying attention)
* Lack of speech causes problems in daily functioning (reduced social and academic verbal participation)

Children with SM may also Demonstrate these Difficulties

(although not diagnostic criteria):

* Reluctance in nonverbal communication, creative/descriptive writing, or gestures
* Anxiety around being the center of attention or focus of others, such as when adults are verbally praising them
* Speech, language, and pragmatic communication weaknesses, even when comfortable
* Other anxieties, fears, and worries
* Hesitancy in using public restrooms or eating in public
* Sensory issues
* Mild social weaknesses or immaturities, possibly due to a lack of experience/ practice
* Anxiety surrounding making choices or advocating for themselves
* Separation issues

It is important to note that some children will not qualify as meeting all criteria for selective mutism, but still have great hesitation to speak or socially engage. Johnson and Wintgens (2016) appropriately label these children as "reluctant speakers." You may be a parent, teacher, or professional reading through this book, and you might notice that the child you are thinking of should not be diagnosed with SM, yet their reluctance to speak impacts them negatively in public interactions, extracurricular activities, social relations, or school participation. Please continue reading and attending to the ideas and worksheets provided; the interventions discussed in this book will be helpful for the vast majority of reluctant speakers.

Both children with SM and reluctant speakers may limit their speech to a whispered voice or a very short verbal response.

If a diagnosis of SM is appropriate for your child, it isn't intended to stigmatize or label them, but instead is the beginning of understanding your child and helping others to understand them and their pattern of strengths and weaknesses. Furthermore, identification of SM allows for treatment in a clinical setting as well as intervention planning in the school setting. Later in the book, we provide more insight into the process for evaluation, diagnosis and intervention planning.

The Good News...

The good news is that there are effective interventions for selective mutism! Research continually demonstrates that the most effective intervention for SM is behavioral treatment using exposure (often referred to as brave practices) (Oerbeck, Stein, Wentzel-Larsen, Langsrud, & Kristensen, 2013; Vecchio & Kearney, 2009). Behavioral interventions are effective in reducing anxiety and increasing verbal communication. In a study on the effectiveness of interventions for SM, the researchers compared behavioral intervention to other treatment types, including medication, family systems therapy, and psychodynamic interventions (Pionek-Stone, Kratochwill, Sladezcek, & Serlin, 2002). The study found that behaviorally-oriented treatments show the largest improvements (Bergman, Gonzalez, Piacentini, & Keller, 2013). Another study found that after behavioral treatment, parents and teachers reported that children had increased their communication, were speaking more at school, and anxiety had decreased. Furthermore, parents can be effective in carrying out this intervention with kids!

Chapter Two

A PARENT'S PERSPECTIVE

I (Shari) am a perfect wife and flawless mother. My children are perfect angels and I cook three-course meals every night for dinner that are elegantly plated and served in a perfectly clean and always organized home. While wearing only the most fashionable clothes in my spotless home, I spend most of my time in the pursuit of my family's happiness (which usually involves Pinterest). OK, absolutely NOT! In reality, we do not eat three-course meals, my kids are amazing (but definitely not angelic), I have no time for Pinterest or even dressing myself and there are many days that I spend thinking repeatedly about bedtime and the relief that comes when the kids are finally tucked in for the night.

If forced to, I might describe myself as a slightly anxious, actively recovering perfectionist. I grew up moving all over the United States as the daughter of a retired Air Force Colonel. I like to think that my early nomadic lifestyle and varied occupations as an adult have helped me to see the world in a unique way and relate to people of all backgrounds. Andrew (my husband) and I have an eight-year-old, Anna, who is overcoming selective mutism and a three-year-old, Emilie, who is overcoming toddlerhood (she is the ultimate "three-nager"!). Each of our children is unique, amazing and challenging in their own way, but both of our girls make us proud (most days)! When Anna was six, she (we) chose to work hard, be brave and take charge of selective mutism. Nothing in my life has been more rewarding than helping Anna find her voice and move past her silence.

Why am I sharing our story so publicly?

I have chosen to share and make public aspects of our family's journey because I know that SM can seem challenging (and it is), but I strongly believe that parents can and should play an active role in helping children overcome SM. As parents, we are in the irreplaceable position to be the most effective influencer of our children. With the right information, tools, support, and patience, over time we can create a team and an environment to affect real change; change that will ultimately steer our children away from their silence, anxiety and fear toward a path of confident connection and rewarding social relationships.

Dr. Kotrba and I decided to join forces and create *Overcoming Selective Mutism: The Parent's Field Guide* because we recognized that there was a distinct void in resources and publications addressing the needs of the caregivers of children with SM. Although there are many excellent and informative books written by experts, including Dr. Kotrba's best-selling first book *Selective Mutism: An Assessment and Intervention Guide for Therapists, Educators, and Parents* and even a handful of books written by those who have overcome SM, there were little to no resources available offering the parent/caregiver perspective. We set out to create a book that more comprehensively addresses the challenges faced by children with SM and their caregivers; a resource guide that would highlight the unique role that parents play as well as provide resources in the form of handouts and practice worksheets. Most importantly, this is the book I would have LOVED to have read when I was struggling to find Anna the help that she needed. We have gone to great lengths to include as many resources and handouts as possible. With that in mind, this book is also an excellent resource for any member of your child's care team – therapists, doctors, teachers, extended family, friends, and caregivers. You will notice that in this chapter, and throughout the book, there are large margins so that you can jot down your thoughts or take notes as you're reading. We also provide "Parent Pointers" with information that we expect to be especially meaningful to parents and "Helpful Handouts" that will assist you in locating worksheets and handouts relevant to the topic being addressed (handouts are located at the end of the chapter unless otherwise noted). Handout and worksheet example pages will be indicated by a blue compass in the top corner while pages that are meant to be interactive will be indicated by a green compass in the top corner.

Because I *AM* a parent, I understand the importance of having effective tools and resources readily available to make the task of helping our children less overwhelming, less time consuming, more manageable and more rewarding. Overcoming selective mutism is a journey. It is a journey for the child but also for the family. For most families, it is so much bigger than getting a child to speak and for many children, including Anna, there are additional challenges that must also be considered.

As the mom of two daughters, my most important mission is to raise them to be independent, secure, and happy children who become independent, secure, happy and contributing adults in the community. It just did not seem enough to simply address Anna's mute behavior. We also needed to address the way in which we managed Anna's related anxiety challenges and systematically teach Anna a more constructive way to approach anxiety-provoking situations. Ours is a journey with many peaks and valleys, successes and setbacks, and we continue onward with the confidence that comes from setting goals, reaching milestones and accomplishing objectives.

Anna the Amazing!

As you read this, please remember that Anna is my sweet first-born baby, so I ask you to indulge my bias. When Anna was little, she was the sweetest, most delicate, and kindest child you could ever meet. She seemed to be born considerate of other children, never taking their toys and always willing to share or give up a toy if another child appeared to "need" it. She had a giggle that would melt your heart and she loved laughing. Anyone lucky enough to hear her and witness it would usually have no choice but to join in. She loved to dress up in costumes and perform plays or dance shows for close family and friends with whom she was comfortable. She took dance, art, and acting classes with her best friends, although she did not talk with the teachers. At times, especially before she was five, she would cry when it was time to separate from me and there were many times when she was unable to participate. We only registered her for classes with her close friends because they seemed to help motivate her to participate even though she was anxious. She was a busy little girl with so many interests.

New experiences were difficult for Anna, but we managed them together. If Anna was having trouble participating at the Karate birthday party, I would join in with her. After she stood for a short time on the sidelines watching, I could usually coax her into trying it with me. Participating in a new activity without me was not something she was ready for until she was closer to 7 years old. I am quite sure there are many acquaintances who must think that I am incredibly enthusiastic about birthday parties. I sure could sell the excitement when I needed to, in order to help Anna join in. Of course, there were times when it did not matter what kind of amazement I was selling - she was not buying! There were days that I could have been pretending to roll around in candy and pet baby unicorns and she still would not have joined me. Looking back, I feel fortunate that she was optimistic enough to want to attend parties and participate non-verbally with my assistance given her level of anxiety.

Understanding Anna's Challenges

From the beginning, Anna was a gentle soul. She literally came out "singing." Andrew and I love to reflect on the moment we first met Anna and recall the sweet sounds she made (she still has an amazing voice!). As she began to grow, however, she seemed to deviate from the normal development patterns we were reading about and from other children we were observing. Although she wasn't necessarily hitting milestones in a timely manner, she would eventually hit them. One of the first major differences that we noticed was that Anna seemed distressed when anyone got excited around her. When our little ones reach an achievement, parents often acknowledge it with excitement and clapping. I assumed this response must be universal, but when Anna was little and we clapped or got excited, she would burst into tears. It seemed to take a good while to calm her down. We began

Don't be afraid to help your child navigate new or scary social situations. Some children need extra help and guidance so they can eventually navigate these situations on their own. There might be someone nearby who thinks you're "helicoptering" and they might even decide to share their opinion with you. Do not let them influence your actions - you know what you need to do to support your child.

It's so important to remember that every child with SM presents differently. While some children are only challenged with overcoming a fear of speaking, others must overcome a host of other challenges. Some children need only basic intervention while others will require the specialized help of an SM expert. Your journey will be uniquely yours.

to more quietly acknowledge her achievements or ignore them altogether. Later we would learn that Anna had sensory sensitivities and she was likely feeling overloaded with auditory input.

As Anna grew older, we started to notice other "quirky" (for lack of a better word) behaviors, which we now believe were rooted in fear, anxiety, and/or perhaps sensory sensitivity. She became more selective about eating and the clothes that she would wear (the more worn and tattered, the better!). We also noticed that she was fearful in situations that did not seem to elicit the same hesitancy from her peers. From bounce houses and tunnels to turning on the water faucet and blowing out birthday candles, Anna seemed to struggle.

When Anna was three, it was my friend's turn to go into the school and read to the children. She called me immediately upon leaving and she said, "It was so weird. Anna completely ignored me and acted like she didn't know who I was." Anna was entirely verbal with my friend in her home and in ours, so this was unusual. Another time, we bumped into our friend and sitter, Dottie, at a store and Anna completely ignored her and wanted to run away. Anna was close to Dottie and spoke quite comfortably with her in most settings; Dottie is essentially like a family member. We were confused. Was this normal behavior that, given time, would pass? Was this something to talk to the pediatrician about?

It seems like a lifetime ago that Anna was struggling in so many ways. I felt helpless and it seemed as though nobody understood Anna enough to guide us through her special challenges. Because SM is relatively rare and most professionals who encounter children with SM (pediatricians, teachers, and even mental health counselors) are unaccustomed to recognizing, diagnosing and treating them, it often goes unrecognized and therefore untreated. In our case, we saw two different psychologists who provided us with alternative explanations for Anna's challenges. The first psychologist believed that Anna might be autistic based on my input and an in-office observation/evaluation. Anna avoided eye contact, was mostly still, would not participate in play activities, and, of course, would not speak. We did not believe autism to be an accurate diagnosis because we knew that Anna was an entirely different child in other settings and situations. The second psychologist visited our home and although Anna never spoke to her, she could see Anna zipping around and presenting quite normally in her interactions with our family. This psychologist told us that Anna was doing fine, she was just extremely shy, and suggested we continue working with her to overcome her motor development delays and sensory challenges. She believed that Anna would "come out of her shell" as she grew older and more confident. Thankfully, Anna's occupational therapist, Angie, helped us to better understand Anna and she encouraged us to seek the appropriate diagnosis of SM.

When Anna was five, we received an official diagnosis of selective mutism. The psychologist who diagnosed her may have overlooked or missed the diagnosis altogether had I not provided information and insight regarding SM. Although she had very little experience with SM, she researched the diagnosis and spoke to experts to confirm our suspicions. We had a formal diagnosis to provide to the school and the psychologist was very clear that we needed to begin treating Anna's SM right away. She believed that the sooner we address it, the better.

We chose to shift Anna's weekly occupational therapy sessions to focus more on her silence and less on motor skill development. At the time, Anna was progressing nicely and making gains in that area, so it was a natural shift. Anna was three when we first began to work with Angie and from the very beginning, Angie had a great rapport with Anna. Anna spoke with Angie right away and Angie seemed to truly understand Anna in a way that helped us lay the groundwork for Anna's "recovery" in the years that followed. Because Angie had successfully treated other children with SM, we felt comfortable that she would help Anna over the SM hurdle as well. Therapy was based on the Developmental Individual-difference Relationship-based (DIR)/Floortime model. Through play and guided games, Anna practiced working through sensory challenges and learning to tolerate anxiety-inducing situations in a safe and fun play space.

Anna's Preschool Years

Anna attended the same school for both the two-year-old and three-year-old programs. Although she seemed quite comfortable at school, she was beside herself every morning when it was time to separate from my husband or me. She did not always attend to morning rituals and oftentimes she was unable (or unwilling) to participate in classroom activities. Anna preferred to be near her teachers although she wouldn't speak to them. The teachers reported that she played with a couple of her classmates and I was assured that she was happy and becoming more independent.

Anna's school loved to include parents in the school community. We were invited quite often to join our little ones for celebrations. I went to every social event because aside from wishing and hoping to enjoy a special day with my sweet girl, Anna did not do well when parents joined in classroom activities. She turned into another little girl altogether, one who seemed unable to control her actions. She was entirely predictable in her unpredictability during classroom celebrations. My sweet baby was the only child losing her cool in any and all ways that you can imagine. I remember trying to determine if it was best to ignore her, reprimand her, spend a few moments in the hall with her, or just call it quits and take her home. I usually did a combination of all those things, feeling completely incompetent. I was certain that I was being judged and labeled as a helicopter mom, an indulgent mom, a cold mom, a weak mom, a mean mom, and/or just a plain old "bad" mom. It was emotional and exhausting caring for Anna in those days. I felt as if I was failing in an area that I so desperately wished to succeed.

When trying to explain occupational therapy, physical therapy, speech therapy, or even a visit to the psychologist's office to your child, it might be best to minimize your explanation of the visit (especially for children 2-5 years of age). For example, occupational therapy may be called "the indoor park." It's a place that involves games, toys and fun with a playmate!

If you are the parent, therapist, teacher, extended family, friend, or doctor of a child with SM, please let the primary caregiver know that they are doing a great job and that you know it's hard work. If you are the primary caregiver, give yourself a break! You are not perfect, nor do you need to be. Keep doing what feels right and seek more knowledge to help your child; that is all that is expected of you. It does get better!

When Anna was almost five, she began a pre-kindergarten child development program at our local public school. It was the first time I was truly able to see Anna's interaction (or lack thereof) with her teachers. The lead teacher, Mrs. Gepford, allowed me to walk Anna into the class every day to help her get settled. Preschool had been drop-off only, so I was not able to see the extent of Anna's anxiety in the classroom. Anna didn't seem to grasp how to unpack her things or complete the other basic morning tasks. In addition, if the teacher tried to engage with her, she would freeze and look away to avoid speaking. With my help in the mornings, Anna finally started most days tear-free, albeit silent.

Mrs. Gepford and her assistant treated Anna with respect and provided her with opportunities to engage without pressuring her to do so. Thankfully, it was in their nature to treat children in a loving, caring and respectful manner. The biggest hurdle during the year was that Anna could not easily be assessed to determine her academic strengths and weaknesses. She was accommodated, but we knew that her lack of speech was abnormal. Coupled with her complete lack of communication with adults in public settings (i.e. grocery store, restaurants, neighbors, etc.), we knew that we needed more help. It was December of that year when we received the SM diagnosis from the psychologist. Based on the diagnosis, we expected Anna to receive specialized help in the school setting. However, nobody at the school had specific knowledge about SM.

With the school unable to provide help, an outside clinician seemed to be our quickest, most direct path to assistance. It was not standard operating procedure to allow outside clinicians into the public classroom but with Mrs. Gepford's enthusiasm to help Anna, we were granted permission! I suggested that Anna's occupational therapist, Angie, could be a "volunteer." Angie filled out the volunteer paperwork and within a few weeks of the background check, Angie began to attend school with Anna for an hour, one day a week. During that time, she brought games and activities that she hoped would allow Anna to open up and have fun with the other students. The ultimate goal was to help Anna feel comfortable enough to speak with Mrs. Gepford. Although Anna had a great time during Angie's visits, she ended the year without ever speaking to her teachers.

As the summer started, we were hopeful. Although Anna hadn't spoken to her teachers during the school year, there were many firsts for her that summer! She began speaking with my sister and her husband for the first time. Anna also had an amazing and important moment conquering a new activity (ice skating) and telling me afterward, "It was really hard mom, but I knew I could try and it would be okay if I fell." In the past, new activities were beyond challenging but this time she was willing to try it and even to fail. Anna was even successful in meeting a couple of new people and speaking with them in our home using a modified "fading" technique (more about this in chapter 5). We still had many challenges ahead of us, but we felt as if we were making some progress.

Mrs. Gepford helped to select Anna's kindergarten teacher early to support the transition to the new school year. She even helped to arrange a meeting with Mrs. Morris over the summer. I knew that this meeting would be pivotal; we wanted to do everything possible to help Anna feel comfortable enough to speak. Building upon Anna's previous success with in-home meetings, we arranged for the first meeting to be in our home. We knew that Anna might freeze if she knew that Mrs. Morris was to be her kindergarten teacher so we didn't tell Anna that she was meeting her teacher. Because Mrs. Morris has two little girls, we told Anna that Emilie (Anna's sister) had a play date with a friend and that Emilie's friend had a sister who would love to play with Anna. We completely removed any expectation surrounding the meeting. In fact, the playdate wasn't even for Anna; it was for her sister!

I prepared Mrs. Morris the best that I could. I asked her to acknowledge Anna but to put more focus on Emilie. I had an activity planned so the kids could work on an art project together. Mrs. Morris was a natural! She has a laid-back personality and she didn't put a lot of demands on Anna right away. Eventually, Anna said a few words to Mrs. Morris by answering questions. After the playdate, Mrs. Morris and I were so excited (although not in front of Anna)! We planned to meet once more at the park/pool a few weeks later. We all had a great time at the pool playdate and Anna continued speaking with Mrs. Morris, although she still didn't let her true personality shine through. After the playdates, I didn't make a big deal about Anna speaking. At the time, Anna didn't like to talk about her fear of speaking and she did not want to acknowledge that it was sometimes difficult to speak.

After the second playdate, I casually mentioned to Anna that Mrs. Morris happened to be a teacher at her school and that Mrs. Morris could be her teacher. The wide grin on Anna's face gave me peace of mind that Anna would be just fine in kindergarten! We planned one more meeting in the classroom with Mrs. Morris and her assistant teacher, Mrs. Joseph, just before school started in August.

An Unexpected Detour

Right before school started, we were set to meet with Mrs. Morris and Mrs. Joseph (the assistant teacher) in the classroom. I had become relaxed because of the early success with Mrs. Morris, and I didn't put as much thought into the classroom meeting as I probably could have. I failed to realize the novelty of the school setting and the addition of a new person could have an effect on Anna's anxiety. I thought that it would be easier if I took Anna to this meeting with her teachers, without her sister. I told Anna we were going to the school to help her teachers get the classroom ready. In retrospect, Emilie would have deflected some attention and it would have been nice to have her along, as she had been included in each previous meeting with Mrs. Morris. I didn't bring an activity because I was afraid of being "pushy." As it turned out, the teachers had a sorting activity

What does "contaminated" mean? When a child regularly avoids speech with a specific person and/or in a specific environment for a long period of time, it can become increasingly difficult to speak to that person or in that environment. Experts in the field of SM refer to this phenomenon as the person or the place being "contaminated."

for Anna. She was asked to test all the markers and determine which ones were no longer working. This activity, while useful, was not a speech-promoting activity (although with the knowledge I have now, I could probably rework the activity to promote speech). In addition, we were in a school setting, a challenging and "contaminated" environment for Anna. There were too many new/challenging variables and Anna did not speak to either teacher during this meeting. The classroom setting, a new person, and attention on Anna during the meeting all likely contributed to an overwhelming situation from which Anna retreated.

Anna's silence at school with her teachers continued for several months despite our best efforts to prevent it. She still struggled socially outside of school as well. Anna would dart away from us and hide if we happened to see any of her school friends around town. She also wouldn't speak with the neighborhood kids at school despite speaking quite normally with them in our neighborhood. Adults outside of our home were entirely out of her scope in terms of speaking. This rigidity in her speaking patterns alarmed us and nobody locally seemed to understand what was happening. We knew that we needed expert help to overcome SM. I had read the books, spoken with other SM moms, and Angie was doing all the right things to help Anna progress, but we still could not break through. We were at a crossroads.

Although we were years into our journey with SM, we found out that Anna still had a long way to go to be fully brave and confident. As her parents, we needed to more fully understand selective mutism.

If you wish to continue the rest of our story now, please turn to Chapter 8. However, we suggest reading along as the book is intended so that our story will be better understood in context.

Chapter Three

THE SELECTIVE MUTISM JOURNEY

While trying to help my daughter, Anna, overcome selective mutism, I started to think of SM as a journey and I imagined myself hiking up a mountain. From first noticing the subtle (and the not-so-subtle) differences between Anna and her peers, to seeking a diagnosis and finding the right resources to help treat her, to participating in therapy, selective mutism felt consuming. Along with enough time and energy, I needed a good map, quality resources/tools, and the right guide to help me find the appropriate path forward.

Dr. Kotrba and I hope you will find practical tools and resources within the field guide to make your journey feel a little less overwhelming. We want you to have easily accessible resources for the situations we know are challenging as a caregiver, educator, and/or clinician. We want you to be able to create a map to guide you on your SM journey and help you to feel more confident in your direction. Ultimately, we hope this book provides the motivation you need to begin.

Before any great journey, it is essential to be prepared; to be knowledgeable about the journey ahead and ready to handle the pitfalls that are likely to emerge. One way to prepare is to heed the advice of others who have taken this journey before. With that in mind, please read through these important lessons learned by those who have navigated a similar path. The advice below was compiled with input from other parents of children with selective mutism, educators, and clinicians. When you feel lost in your journey (which will undoubtedly happen), please take a deep breath, find something funny to laugh at, relax, and re-read these points!

Prepare for Your Journey

1. **Put on your oxygen mask before helping others:**
   Simplify and DO NOT feel guilty! Raising any child requires energy, patience and love. Raising a child with special emotional, developmental or physical needs can seem especially consuming. The additional energy, patience, love and focus required is often underestimated and, as parents, we tend to discount how quickly these extra efforts add up. We often overschedule without setting aside time to recharge and, in turn, we feel drained and exhausted.

   ☀ Give yourself permission to slow down and simplify your life. Do not feel guilty for prioritizing your family.

- Tell yourself, "I'm not going to organize my closet this month/year. Maybe next month/year I'll have more time for that."
- Don't fear saying no! "I won't be able to help with the fundraising auction this year. Maybe next year or perhaps in the Spring I'll have more time."
- Avoid taking on additional work projects (if that is an option for you).

2. **Have a plan:**

Stay focused and organized to assist your child in reaching their goals. We've all heard the mantra, "Failing to plan is planning to fail." As much as we would like to pretend that isn't true, we know it makes sense and that having a plan will ultimately help us to reach our goals. In this book we will provide insight, knowledge and tools that will assist you in planning, organizing and taking action. Of course, life doesn't always go according to plan, it's okay to attend to other pressing matters or take a brief break but return to your plan as soon as you are able.

3. **The early bird gets the worm:**

The earlier SM is recognized, addressed and treated, the better! Growing evidence suggests that, in general, helping a 6-year-old with SM is easier than treating a 14-year-old. If your child is older, please understand that treatment may be harder, but it is certainly not impossible.

- SM is not as difficult to treat as it was once believed to be. With early intervention and practice, we should expect to help our children move beyond silence.
- If progress seems impossible, don't be afraid to try any and all tools in the arsenal, including medication.

4. **Be consistent:**

Gain perspective and a better understanding of your child's behavior and motivations, and then adjust your expectations of, and your reactions to, their behavior. We need to better determine when to be firm and when to be a little more relaxed. It is helpful to view our children's behaviors (especially those that we deem as negative) as actions not meant to be vindictive, bad or hurtful. We should always assume that our child is a good kid making an unhelpful choice (and potentially an uncontrollable choice) and communicate with them in this manner. They should know that we love them, we believe in them, and that they are AMAZING before we can discuss their behavior. Even when we assume their behavior is due to stress and/or anxiety, it's critical we provide consistent and relevant consequences balanced with empathy. Inconsistent consequences are especially confusing for kids and may, in fact, be anxiety-provoking. We must teach our children that it is acceptable to feel anxious, mad, sad, or angry but it is not acceptable to hit, kick, scream, or throw as a result. From an early age, consequences should be expected.

Some children with selective mutism may present as challenging, strong willed, or even oppositional. See Chapter 9 for more information and helpful tips to help manage challenging behaviors.

5. **Expect forward momentum:**

Imagine that we are hiking up a steep mountain. Suddenly, the weather gets bad and we must stop halfway. At first, we are grateful for the rest and feeling somewhat better. But after several days, we are getting antsy. We've cut into our rations, our climbing muscles are weakening, we are cold and wet, and we are beginning to fear for the future. Stagnating may keep us from ever reaching the top. The same is true of the SM journey. If we stop moving forward, we are not just standing still but rather sliding back. Kids begin to forget how to push past the feeling of discomfort. Therefore, if you feel you have hit a plateau, DO NOT STAY STUCK. Plan small yet consistent steps forward at all times because "brave muscles" must be stretched, flexed, and consistently worked for them to be ready for action when the time comes.

- ❋ EXPECT consistent, even if slow, improvement. (Keep in mind, this doesn't mean there won't be an occasional setback along the way.)
- ❋ Many clinicians, if they don't have experience with SM, will not understand that our kids can and will make progress (SLOW is ok, but NO progress is not)
- ❋ Kids with SM need to get comfortable with their feelings of unease and anxiety. The more opportunities they have to push through their fear, the more likely they will learn how to cope. If they stay in their comfort zone and aren't pushed to continue progressing, they are not able to capitalize on forward momentum.

6. **Heads or tails:**
Avoid the **headwinds** and take advantage of **tailwinds**! We all know that when our children are sick, hungry, and/or tired it is difficult for them to focus. Additionally, some children become quite cranky and more likely to meltdown. This is not the time to push our children to take on new challenges. Timing is everything! Avoid almost certain failure by timing your requests appropriately.

- ❋ Do not push for new accomplishments during times of unexpected or profound life change. Expect that progress might even slow down.
- ❋ After a taxing playdate, it might be best to avoid more practice at the grocery store.
- ❋ When children are sick and feeling miserable, give them a break!

Just because our children are making progress and are more able to participate in social situations does not mean that it's easy for them to do so. In addition, being able to speak easily with one person does not make it easy for them to speak to *all* people. Our children may come home from school exhausted from their efforts. They will likely be more "taxed" than a child who does not have SM or social anxiety. They may need extra time to relax and unwind before we put additional demands on them, especially in the beginning. It is okay to give them the time and space they need to recharge.

7. **Communication is important:**
It is so important to communicate effectively with our children (Chapter 4 provides additional guidance). They are likely aware of their trouble speaking,

but they probably have no idea what to do about it. Our role is to observe without judging and to help them make sense of what's happening. We can help children to realize that everyone has challenges and that is what makes us all unique. Knowing when and how to start the conversation can be difficult. Use the conversation starters below to help:

* "That seemed hard. Do you want to talk about it?"
* "You seemed a little uncomfortable when the waiter asked what you wanted."
* "Your teacher tells me that you have a hard time answering her questions."

Good follow-up questions might be:

* "How does that make you feel?"
* "Do you want to tell me more about that?"
* "Why do you think…?"

8. **One size does not fit all:**
Every child will require a different path forward. The journey will be different for each and every child and family. It is important to understand that while each child may exhibit a reluctance to speak, the cause for their anxiety and the ways in which they respond to treatment are likely to be very different. It is not only important for parents to understand this distinction but also for therapists, teachers, and anyone who may have first-hand knowledge of another child with SM. It is easy to fall into the trap of believing that because *Nancy* had SM and she "grew out of it" by the fourth grade, *Joe* will also just "grow out of it." As an outsider, we have no idea what kind of help *Nancy* had to "grow out of it" or whether she had any co-existing factors playing into her diagnosis. *Overcoming Selective Mutism: The Parent's Field Guide* is intended for caregivers, therapists, and school personnel who are motivated to create a relevant path forward, taking into consideration all aspects of the child's strengths and weaknesses as well as any external factors that might come into play.

9. **The balancing act:**
It's much easier to balance on a beam than it is to balance on a tight rope! Raising children is a balancing act. While most parents are balancing on a beam and struggling from time to time to stay on top, parents of children with special needs (SM included) can feel as if we are balancing on a tight rope. We did not sign up for the tight rope walk, but nevertheless we are raising children and making choices that will cause us to lean and teeter on the edge. We may correct our posture only to find ourselves re-balancing again a few moments, days, or even years later. It's difficult to feel secure in our decisions.

I, Shari, find it helpful to remember that we are just as capable as the parent down the street who seems to be raising a social "all-star." Our efforts and our child's successes may go unnoticed now, but when they become confident and secure adults, contributing in the best way that they are able, we will be just as proud! My husband always jokes, "I'm a second-half player." Coming in off the bench provides just as much of an opportunity to make an impact and to succeed. It isn't where our children start, but where they end up!

10. You are your child's champion:

You are your child's best advocate! Don't be afraid to ask for and make changes!

* Although well intentioned, doctors, psychologists, teachers, and administrators (your team) are not always right. It's best to frequently and openly discuss any concerns you have in an effort to help your child receive the support they need.

* In school and in the community, you must be your child's advocate and that may require a few uncomfortable requests or conversations. Take deep breaths, seek input from others, prepare your thoughts and words carefully, and then make your intentions clear while remaining respectful. Your child comes first and, at times, that may upset the apple cart, but if you approach the situation carefully and with respect, your request is more likely to be followed through.

* Caregivers, remember that the intervention team will be working with you and they want your child to succeed, too. The more information and resources you can provide, the more likely they are to listen. There are many great handouts and resources within this book!

If you are at the beginning of your journey, struggling along the way, or even confident in your direction, we hope you will continue your journey using *The Parent's Field Guide* to:

☑ Simplify the process for helping children overcome SM
☑ Feel empowered and confident in setting your path forward
☑ Learn proven tools and strategies to help your child make progress on their journey to overcome SM
☑ Understand that it's about so much more than simply getting kids to speak

Introducing *"The Field Map™"*

We created *The Field Map* as a visual representation of the SM journey including the elements we feel are fundamental to helping children find their voice. This map will provide an overview of the journey to come. On the following pages, you will become acquainted with the appearance and the concepts represented on *The Field Map* and how you might use the map to devise a plan for your child. As the book progresses, we will slowly provide more detail about each element and its importance in overcoming SM. Chapters 5 and 7 will provide several handouts and worksheets to help you plan your child's journey in a way that is motivating, fun, and engaging for you and your child.

Remember that your child may also feel like they are navigating the world on a tightrope rather than a beam! Most children will experience struggles and they may feel as though their life is a balancing act, but children with SM will likely feel this more acutely. It's important to recognize this tendency and to support them when we notice them starting to falter.

*Reminder: We don't live in a world of "should." The teacher **should** know about SM. The school counselor **should** help your child. My child **should** talk to others without all these steps. **Should** will not get us where we want to be. We must be proactive. If your child isn't being optimally "served" even after your best efforts to inform others about SM, you may need to find new allies and make new plans.*

Overcoming Selective Mutism

The Field Map™

Peers Peak   **School Summit**   **Community Crest**

Mount Mindful   Challenge Pathway   **Victory Valley**   **Foundational Foothills**

Tools for Communication Success
Specific strategies used to promote speech.

(1) Rapport Building (2) Verbal Prompting
(3) Stimulus Fading (4) Shaping (5) Medical Intervention

Pathway Hazards
Factors that may influence difficulty level and progress toward conquering challenges.

(1) The Audience
(2) The Environment
(3) The Speech Demand

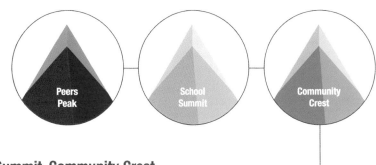

The Mountains (Domains): Peers Peak, School Summit, Community Crest

Overarching challenges that children with selective mutism face in speaking to peers, speaking at school, and speaking with community members. To reach the top of these peaks might require conquering several challenge pathways.

Challenge Pathway

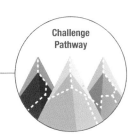

A planned, step-wise, and structured approach to conquering challenges. Challenge pathways provide the small steps needed to move your child from their current level of engagement to comfortable speech. Determining which intermediate steps will assist a child to reach a particular goal or milestone is truly the key to overcoming selective mutism. Challenge pathways should be planned with careful thought and consideration of the child's current abilities and challenges.

Foundational Foothills

A solid foundation is paramount for the successful intervention/treatment of selective mutism. Educate and prepare yourself, your child and your family. Build and educate a team of "helpers" (school, therapist, family, community, etc.).

Mount Mindful

Key skills that do not directly address a child's inability to speak but skills that if mastered, may be beneficial in helping to change the child's mindset – helping them to be more aware of their thoughts and how those thoughts may impact their actions.

- The problem with perfection
- The importance of sticking with challenges (grit)
- The more you do, the more you can do
- Recognizing and managing discomfort

Victory Valley

Victory Valley represents accomplishment over fear, strength in facing discomfort, the conquering of challenges, and bravery in taking small steps toward larger "victories". Achievements should be celebrated!

You may find that some steps and examples are integral to helping your child, while other advice may seem foreign and unnecessary. That is to be expected! You and your child's journey will be different than those taken by other families of children with SM, but you are not alone.

Throughout the book, we highlight several challenge pathways. Notice that each pathway begins with the easiest step at the bottom and progresses toward the top with the final most challenging step.

The Mountains (Domanins)

Overarching challenges facing children with SM

Generally speaking, there are three main overarching challenges facing children with SM – speaking with **peers**, speaking in the **community**, and speaking at **school**. On *The Field Map*, you'll notice that we prominently display three mountains, *Peers Peak*, *Community Crest*, and *School Summit* (corresponding to those main challenges). If you think about your child's abilities/challenges in this context as you read through the rest of the book, you can begin to think in terms of where the "work" might begin. We will refer to these three overarching challenges as "domains."

Challenge Pathway

A planned step-wise approach to conquering challenges

In order to overcome any type of fear or anxiety, an individual must face that fear in small steps. Facing fears in small steps allows for a slow decrease in anxiety, as well as increased confidence and feelings of accomplishment. In other texts, these slow steps toward facing fears are referred to as a "fear hierarchy." We chose to refer to them as *challenge pathways* because they illustrate specific, planned steps on a path to overcoming challenges (big and small). The more often children take pathways that truly challenge them, the more likely they are to forge a path toward overcoming selective mutism.

Learning To Drive

Challenge Pathway Example

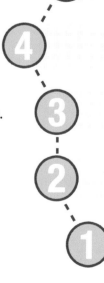

Driving on the road independently.

Driving on the road with a parent in the car supervising.

Driving on the road with a parent in the car providing instructions.

Driving in an empty parking lot with a parent in the car.

Learning the parts of a car and the steps for driving.

Placing money directly into the clerk's hand and accepting change back in hand.

Placing money directly into the clerk's hand, and accepting change that is placed on the counter.

Holding cash out for the clerk to take.

Placing money on the counter for the clerk to pick up.

Pathway Hazards

Factors impacting the difficulty of the challenge and the child's ability to conquer it

Pathway Hazards are factors which may affect your child's ability to reach a given goal, whether it be with peers, in the community or at school. There are three main categories for *Pathway Hazards* – the audience, the environment, and the speech demand involved in the challenge.

- **The Audience** – How many people are there? Are they particularly difficult to speak with? Might they be contaminated? Is there a perceived audience for speech? Does my child do better with or without a parent in the room? Are men vs. women easier? Peers vs. adults?
- **The Environment** – Is this a place where the child is used to speaking or used to not speaking? Is it a new environment? Is it chaotic or quiet? Is the environment associated with a significant speech expectation? Is there anything about the environment that might make it challenging for the child to speak?
- **The Speech Demand** – Is the child being asked to respond (typically easier) or initiate (typically harder)? How lengthy of a response is expected or needed to answer the question? Is the response scripted (e.g., using forced-choice questions, reading, or a game with very defined responses like "Go Fish")? Does the child understand the question? Is it an easy, concrete question or a more abstract one (e.g., naming would be concrete and easy, while questions requesting opinions on topics are more abstract and may be harder)?

Children may be hesitant to respond to a question if they believe additional questions or a conversation may follow.

When considering which challenge your child may be ready to take on, think about the *Pathway Hazards* as they might be helpful in determining the appropriate order of steps to reach important goals. Children with SM can be very sensitive to environmental and situational factors; a small shift or change in these factors may change the outcome of a child's progress along a *challenge pathway*.

Foundational Foothills

Setting the foundation for your intervention

Before you embark on any great journey, you must make sure the foundation is solid. We take great care to make sure you are informed and prepared before exploring specific intervention methods. Establishing a foundation includes educating and preparing your child and family for the intervention, as well as building and educating your intervention team (school, therapist, family, etc.).

Mount Mindful

Important life skills that may benefit children with SM

Further off in the distance, you'll notice *Mount Mindful*. Despite its placement in the background, *Mount Mindful* provides important insight into key skills that are significant for all children (and especially those with SM). These are not necessarily skills that will directly address your child's inability to speak, but they are skills that may change the way in which they perceive their own anxiety and the struggles they face as they move forward toward overcoming their challenges. There is no perfect time to begin introducing these concepts to children. We suggest you take any and all opportunities to teach these important lessons:

- **The problem with perfection**: Children with SM often fear being imperfect (which may garner more attention and perhaps ridicule). They may go to great lengths to avoid being perceived as imperfect. By demonstrating our own comfort with making mistakes – perhaps even purposefully making mistakes ourselves – we model how mistakes are expected, are a part of human nature, and how they can be a learning experience. We discuss ways to address the perfection problem in Chapter 9.
- **The importance of sticking with challenges (grit)**: Not giving up during times of stress and anxiety is an incredibly important characteristic and it is a skill that can be learned and practiced. In recent years, grit has been touted as one of the key indicators for success in life. For more on grit, see Chapter 4.
- **The more you do, the more you can do**: Forward momentum through small, but courageous, steps will add to a child's sense of bravery and success. It is easy to become frustrated with slow movement on challenge pathways; however, celebrating even small accomplishments can help propel children forward. One way that parents can encourage forward momentum is through reward systems, which we review in Chapter 4.

- ☀ **Recognizing and managing discomfort**: A key step in facing fear is realizing that the signal is discomfort, NOT danger. Being brave and courageous includes doing what is important despite the discomfort. Thus, it is important to encourage kids to predict discomfort, understand that it is a false alarm, and move forward toward the goal they set out to achieve. In other words, we hope children learn how to be comfortable being uncomfortable!

The Backpack "Tools"

Strategies to promote speech

Don't forget the backpack! It has all the "tools" you will need to successfully navigate challenge pathways. These evidence-based techniques and interventions are researched and proven to help children overcome selective mutism. In Chapter 5, you will learn more about each of the tools represented in the backpack including Rapport Building, Verbal Prompting, Stimulus Fading, Shaping, and Medical Intervention.

Victory Valley

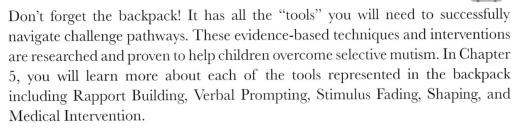

Along the way, there will be many challenges but there will also be many victories – some small and some mighty! It can be very motivating for children to see how far they have come. This part of the field map was designed for "bragging rights." You can use stickers, markers, crayons, etc. to commemorate accomplishment over fear, challenge pathways conquered, and other examples of bravery as your child takes small steps toward larger victories! Chapter 4 will provide more information on Victory Valley as well as a handout that you and/or your child may use to keep track of accomplishments..

Chapter Four

SETTING THE FOUNDATION FOR AN EFFECTIVE INTERVENTION

Building the foundation for an effective intervention and ultimately claiming victory over selective mutism will take on different forms for different families. In the previous chapter, we provided a high-level, "bird's eye view" of the journey to overcome SM with the *Field Map*. It's time to dive a little deeper into each of the components presented on the map. In this chapter we focus on the Foundational Foothills, Mount Mindful, and Victory Valley.

A Strong Foundation will Often Include:

- **A guide** (usually a therapist) to help you better navigate new and challenging pathways. They will help lessen the difficulty of the journey and they may even uncover a few shortcuts!
- **Being prepared** is also vital. You must prepare yourself, your child, your family and other team members for the intervention process (the journey!). Perhaps the most important aspect of preparation is building an understanding of SM and establishing the importance of working toward bravery with speaking.

If you believe that your child may struggle with some or all the criteria of SM, it is recommended that an official diagnosis be made. A formal diagnosis can open the door to effective treatment, interventions and accommodations in the school setting, and a better overall understanding of the child, as well as set the foundation for your intervention "team."

Finding a Knowledgeable Guide

Many parents find it helpful to consult first with their child's pediatrician about their concerns and to rule out developmental delays or physical issues. Some physicians are not familiar with selective mutism; it may be helpful to bring information about SM to the appointment. After consulting with the pediatrician, parents are encouraged to find a treating professional who can provide diagnosis and treatment. Helpful treating professionals may include:

Child Psychologist – a doctoral-level mental health professional. In the context of SM, they work to address anxiety and related issues, and preferably have several years of experience treating children with behavioral or cognitive-behavioral therapy. Psychologists understand how to incorporate both emotional and behavioral components into their treatment protocol. They can be helpful in diagnosing SM, conducting brave practices (exposures), consulting with the school, and training/supporting parents.

Psychiatrist – a physician with a specialty in mental health diagnosis and medical intervention, including prescribing medication for anxiety. They can be helpful in diagnosing SM and considering medical intervention. They are especially important if parents are concerned about medication due to co-existing medical issues (e.g., diabetes) or if there are multiple medications prescribed.

Psychotherapist/Counselor – a masters-level mental health professional, with similarities in training to psychologists. Counselors may also be helpful in diagnosing SM, using behavioral treatment, consulting with the school, and training/supporting parents with intervention.

Speech-Language Pathologist (SLP) – a professional who has training and experience in evaluating and treating children who have speech and language weaknesses. They may be helpful in targeting specific speech/language weaknesses and treating children with co-occurring speech issues, and may also be an important interventionist for increasing speech through brave practices.

Occupational Therapist (OT) – a professional who helps children to do things that are important and meaningful tasks of daily living such as eating, dressing, school activities, and work. They may work with the child on scaffolding (moving children slowly through difficult tasks), becoming comfortable with discomfort via motor and experiential activities, and addressing additional challenges including processing and sensory issues.

Many factors go into the final decision of selecting an appropriate therapist including physician referral, insurance, cost of treatment, and distance from home. When trying to determine which treating professional will be the best fit for your child, don't be afraid to call them and ask questions about their background and experience with SM and childhood anxiety. In addition to having clinical knowledge, the therapist must be able to build rapport with your child. As a parent, you will also want to feel comfortable with the therapist and feel as though the therapist values you as an essential part of your child's SM journey.

Finding your guide
How to find the right treating professional.

What are the qualities of an ideal guide?

IDEAL	NOT IDEAL and/or NOT EFFECTIVE
Offers exposure-based behavioral therapy	Play therapy, psychodynamic therapy, art therapy
Experience working with SM (at least 5-10 previous patients is preferable)	Little to no experience working with SM, and unwilling to thoroughly learn or consult with an expert
Is willing to consult with the school and/or attend school meetings	Unwilling to consult with school/shows little interest in helping parents advocate at school
Provides parent training	Parents are not invited to be involved
Seems to be a good personality match for your child	Does NOT seem to be a good match for your child and/or does not build adequate rapport in a timely manner
Has a plan for increasing speech, even if the child does not talk to them at first	Believes they are unable help, if the child cannot talk to them
Is willing and able to practice brave work outside of the office in a wide variety of community settings	Is NOT flexible and motivated to meet the child at their current ability level.

When seeking a therapist, parents might ask the following questions:

1. How many children with selective mutism have you treated?

2. What treatment strategies do you use for kids with SM? *(answer should include practices/exposures)*

3. Are you able to provide exposure experiences outside of the office setting?

4. How do you involve the parent and school in your intervention?

5. What do you do if the child doesn't talk to you in the first few sessions? *(answer should include a specific plan for eliciting speech as opposed to allowing the child to start speaking when they are ready or providing a referral to a different treatment source)*

There are many excellent and capable providers who are simply unable to leave their office setting for school meetings and community practice due to legal and regulatory reasons. Some of the best therapists can be handcuffed by limitations but in most cases find creative ways to continue to support, train and guide parents nevertheless. Expert treating professionals can successfully guide their patients in spite of these constraints.

What if you can't find an ideal provider in your area?

Many parents may find that they are unable to find all of these qualities in a provider in their area. While it might be best to work with a professional who has experience with successfully treating children with SM, another option is to look for therapists who are trained in behavioral therapy and work regularly with children with anxiety. These therapists might be able and willing to obtain more training specifically in selective mutism, allowing them to modify their approach to treat your child. It's important that the therapist is willing, if necessary, to consult with an SM expert in the event that progress stalls.

Some families choose to travel to see a clinician experienced in SM due to a lack of availability of quality therapeutic support locally or because their child presents with a particularly challenging case of SM. By traveling to an expert, the child can see a therapist with years of experience treating SM, and in most cases the expert will consult with the school and family throughout treatment. Within the SM community, traveling to an expert for an evaluation and a "concentrated-dose" of behavioral treatment is often referred to as an "intensive intervention."

Intensive Intervention for SM

When psychologists are treating any type of specific anxiety or phobia, the "special sauce" for the intervention is consistent and repeated exposure to that fear. Without consistent and repeated exposure, children will take much longer (or may never be able to) feel comfortable in anxiety-provoking situations (i.e., desensitization). For several years, practitioners have been using more "concentrated-dose" interventions to treat all different types of anxiety, from specific phobias to panic disorder. Concentrated doses, or "intensives," allow the child to face challenges more quickly and build success upon success in a short period of time. Treatment time may be shortened because the therapist is able to build upon momentum, which saves precious weeks, months, and years of possible avoidance and silence. While the up-front cost is likely to be higher, the cost of a one-week intensive intervention might be less expensive compared over time to one year of weekly therapy sessions. Clinical evidence is demonstrating that intensive intervention not only shortens the overall time of intervention required but also the hours of brave practices necessary (Kurtz, 2013).

A single session during an intensive intervention may last anywhere from 2-5 hours. Typically, intensives consist of 3-5 consecutive days of these longer treatment sessions. The child's ability to maintain energy and focus should be considered in determining the length of a session. Parent finances may also be a consideration, as most insurance companies will not pay for more than "treatment as usual" (one 60-minute session per day). Another consideration may be a family's proximity to a qualified treating professional. Families that are driving longer distances for treatment will often need to spend more focused time with the therapist to achieve preliminary goals and develop a "map" for success upon returning home.

There are several options for "intensive" intervention, and the *goal* of the intervention may affect which option a family chooses:

- **Individualized intensive treatment sessions at a therapist's office**, with one-on-one behavioral treatment, parent training, and community practice. Longer treatment sessions may reduce the overall duration of treatment and may allow for more brave practice opportunities in one day, such as practicing a scavenger hunt in the office, followed by a scavenger hunt in Home Depot (with novel adults), and then ordering ice cream as a reward for the child's hard work. Rather than waiting a full week (or more) in between sessions, intensive sessions are scheduled for multiple days in a row. This reduces warm-up time and allows for possibly faster progression toward speech. Good intensive interventions have a parent-training component to help parents understand how to effectively elicit speech across settings, plan brave practices, and reward brave work. Parent training should also support parents in advocating for their child in the school setting.

- **Intensive treatment sessions in the school setting**, conducted by a therapist. In-school intensives may involve behavioral treatment for most of the school day, over several days. Goals might include working with teachers, staff, and peers to elicit speech, and practice brave talking in multiple school environments. The school-based intensive approach may also reduce warm-up time, allow for possibly faster progression toward speech, and may reduce the potential disruptions to the child's school schedule that long-term intervention involves. In-school intensives are incredibly useful in both intervening directly in the child's school, where the anxiety usually occurs, and at the same time training the staff on how to successfully interact with the child. However, these in-school intensives may not have a parent-training component, and finding a therapist who can travel to the school (and become licensed in a different state, if necessary) may be difficult. Conducting an intensive intervention in the school requires a (sometimes lengthy) planning and approval process; in order for the intensive intervention to be effective, the school must provide a private space to begin the intervention, provide teachers' schedules for brave practice opportunities, and allow the child to be pulled from the classroom during the intervention. The school may also have requests, such a background check for the therapist or parental consent for any other children who may be involved in the intervention.

- **Intensive group treatment.** Summer camps and weekly groups are available nationally for children with SM. The goal of these camps and groups is to simulate a classroom setting and allow the child to practice their brave behaviors with peers and adults in a group setting. Camps such as Confident Kids Camp© (*www.confidentkidscamp.com*) are organized to

Parents looking for providers in their area might look at the Selective Mutism Association (SMA) website under "Find Help" or reach out to other parents on social media (e.g., Facebook support groups). In addition to the list of providers posted on the SMA website there is a list of state coordinators who might be able to help point you toward experienced professionals in your community. Although these referral networks may be helpful, it is important to personally evaluate the treating provider to be certain that they have appropriate experience and will be an ideal fit for your child.

allow the child to practice anxiety-provoking school and public situations, such as responding to the teacher's questions, show-and-tell and oral presentations, ordering at an ice cream store, and participating verbally in group projects. Each child is paired with their own "camp counselor" – a trained adult who provides individualized support throughout the week. Camp provides a child with an opportunity for brave practice right before the start of a new school year or during other breaks from school, and many children experience a large increase in speech during the week of camp and maintenance of those gains into the new school year. Camps offer intensive practice with no real disruption to the child's schedule (as most camps take place over the summer), provide direct peer practice, and allow parents and children to meet other families also working to overcome SM. A list of nation-wide camps and groups can be found on the Selective Mutism Association's website at *www.selectivemutism.org*.

It is important to note that for many families, intensive interventions aren't a stand-alone solution. They often provide an amazing boost in progress, build confidence in the child and family, and help train the parent and school quickly on the intervention plan. Nevertheless, follow-up after the intensive is almost always necessary either via phone consultations with the therapist who conducted the intensive or in-person behavioral therapy with a local therapist (perhaps in consultation with the expert). Some families find it helpful to have more than one intensive, such as doing an in-school week-long intensive to focus on obtaining more speech in school and training the school staff, and then attending a summer camp to revive brave work skills and obtain more peer practice before school starts.

There are many intensive intervention options for children older than 8; however, making the decision to take part in this type of treatment, with an older child, is something to consider carefully and in consultation with a highly qualified treating professional.

Children who have expressed some interest in speaking more, children who are young (and therefore typically easier to treat), and/or children who have already made some progress toward speech are generally excellent candidates for an intensive intervention. An intensive intervention *alone* may not be a good fit if your child tires easily, is older (many professionals consider children older than age 8 to be more difficult to treat), demonstrates severe SM symptoms, or absolutely refuses to engage in treatment. For these children, weekly behavioral treatment combined with school intervention and parent training might be the best beginning intervention plan.

Once you decide on a treatment option and a therapist, scheduling a diagnostic appointment is an important next step.

Evaluation and Diagnosis of Selective Mutism

A typical evaluation might include the following components:
1. **An extensive interview with parents**, including obtaining developmental and medical history along with current symptoms. The most important

component to this evaluation is understanding the factors that influence WHERE the child speaks ("The Environment"), TO WHOM the child speaks ("The Audience"), and HOW the child communicates ("The Speech Demand"). We refer to these factors as Pathway Hazards because they can influence the difficulty level or the ability of the child to verbally engage. Establishing a baseline of the factors that influence your child's comfort level with speech, before treatment occurs, will be helpful for planning the intervention.

2. **Questionnaires about anxiety, behavior, and SM.** It is likely that the therapist will request that parents, teachers, and other caregivers fill out the questionnaires to obtain a more global perspective of speech and behavior.

3. **A teacher interview and/or observation in the classroom**. Because school is typically the most challenging environment for children to speak, it is important to have a clear picture of their behavior and quality of speech in the school setting.

4. **Videos of the child:** Provide videos of your child in their home environment, in the classroom and in community environments with communication partners. Having access to quick snapshots of the child at their most comfortable and at their least comfortable enables the therapist to get a sense of your child's current abilities and severity of symptoms.

5. **Historical data about the child**. Parents are encouraged to bring in past reports from psychologists, psychiatrists, school psychologists, occupational therapists, and speech-language pathologists, teachers' notes or past grade cards, data about previous evaluations or interventions (i.e., behavioral data taken during a school observation or clinical notes from previous interventions), and/or charts or worksheets parents have used in the past for behavioral change (e.g., reward charts).

6. **A direct structured observation**. Christopher Kearney (2006) describes behavioral observations as the "key lynchpin" of assessment and treatment of SM. They can confirm or rule out selective mutism, point to co-existing diagnoses, suggest the severity of speech reluctance, and guide the intervention. We recommend a structured observation in a school or clinical setting, involving the parent (or another adult with whom the child feels comfortable enough to speak). More information on how therapists can conduct a direct structured observation can be found in Dr. Kotrba's book, *Selective Mutism: An Assessment and Intervention Guide for Therapists, Educators, and Parents.*

7. **A feedback session with intervention planning.** In this separate session, the psychologist or therapist should sit down with parents, discuss the outcomes and findings of the evaluation, and connect these findings with research-based treatment plans.

It is strongly recommended that parents sign a "Disclosure Form" between the therapist and the school, allowing the therapist to obtain information from and collaborate directly with the school. Your therapist should provide this form at the beginning of the evaluation or treatment.

Cataloguing Current Speaking Abilities & Challenges

The Audience, The Environment, and the Speech Demand

Current Abilities

With whom does the child speak, in which locations does the interaction take place, and how does your child respond to that person?

The Audience	The Environment	The Speech Demand
With whom will the child currently speak? (e.g. grandma, aunt, friends, cousins, classmates, coaches, etc.)	In what environments will they currently speak to this person? (e.g. home, school hallway, their home, church, car, etc.)	How does the child communicate with this person? (e.g. gestures, writing, whispers, one-word responses, respond vs. initiate, etc.)

Current Challenges

In general (and in most cases), which factors present challenges for the child?

The Audience

Size of Audience
- ❏ One-on-one
- ❏ Small group
- ❏ Large group/public speaking

Familiarity of Audience
- ❏ Novel (new) people
- ❏ Familiar people
- ❏ Contaminated people

Gender
- ❏ Men
- ❏ Women

Age
- ❏ Adults
- ❏ Children

The Environment

Familiarity with Environment
- ❏ Novel (new) place
- ❏ Familiar place
- ❏ Contaminated place

Perceived Privacy
- ❏ Closed/private space
- ❏ Open/public

Other Environmental Factors
- ❏ Crowded/chaotic place
- ❏ Noisy place

The Speech Demand

Length/Type of Speech
- ❏ Short responses
- ❏ Longer responses
- ❏ Asking a question
- ❏ Starting a conversation
- ❏ Asking for help
- ❏ Maintaining a conversation

Sound/Volume of Speech
- ❏ Making sounds
- ❏ Whispering
- ❏ Using a full voice

Expectation/Comfort Level
- ❏ Concrete or automatic answers (e.g. age, name, etc.)
- ❏ Planned, scripted, and/or practiced speech
- ❏ Unexpected, unplanned and/or spontaneous speech
- ❏ Greetings and polite words

After a diagnosis of selective mutism or social anxiety is confirmed, the real work begins. Hopefully you have now added a "guide" to your team – a therapist who is able to provide knowledgeable information, recommendations, and intervention. An important next step in the work of parents, teachers, and professionals is truly understanding the impact and nature of avoidance in selective mutism. Children feel anxious, fearful, or uncomfortable when they perceive a prompt to speak or engage, and therefore **they take action to avoid that feeling of discomfort.** While many adults and peers can become disheartened and even hurt by the fact that a child does not speak to them, please understand that the child is not avoiding a person out of dislike or disinterest. In fact, many children don't speak to their very favorite people! Instead, they are specifically avoiding the *discomfort* that follows a prompt to speak or engage. When they avoid, they are typically rescued – parents speak for them, a sibling answers for them, friends tell the teacher what they need, or others simply stop asking them questions that would require a verbal answer. This is usually done to help the child because it is clear they are uncomfortable, and others want to protect them. This feels like a relief for the child with selective mutism; they have avoided an uncomfortable interaction and they feel much better.

Throughout this journey, parents are encouraged to take care of their own emotional wellbeing. Ideas for self-care include relaxation, meditation, exercise, building a strong social network, reaching out for help, taking time out to re-energize, and planning enjoyable activities.

Anxiety is temporary and harmless, but avoidance can last a lifetime. When we allow and even encourage our children to avoid speaking, we aren't helping them at all! Instead, we are perpetuating a belief that they are unable to handle these situations and that being rescued is a better alternative. Adults should focus on small, incremental steps for children to learn new skills.

Retraining the Brain

Helping your child build distress tolerance and grit

Learning to tolerate distress is an incredibly important skill for children to develop. At times, parents (perhaps unknowingly) cause their children to feel distressed in order to secure positive long-term outcomes. At a young age, parents leave their children alone to sleep in their crib or in the care of others. This may be upsetting for the child but doing so teaches them to self-soothe and they learn that it is okay to sleep and play independent of their parents. When children are taken for vaccinations and medical treatments they might also feel distressed, but those necessary experiences serve to protect them from illness. At some point, parents must begin disciplining their children for poor choices. When a child is not getting their way, they certainly feel distressed but by allowing them to "own" their distress, they are learning self-control, how to cope with disappointment, and how to follow through on directions.

The experiences highlighted above are commonplace and necessary but as a parent, they can be painful to observe! It can be difficult (anxiety provoking and perhaps embarrassing) to watch our children suffer, cry, throw a tantrum, or take on challenging hurdles without stepping in to save them. However, we do a disservice to them by rescuing them from situations that they are likely capable of handling. Researcher Angela Duckworth examined characteristics of children who were the most "successful" – those who did the best at school, socially, and in the working world later in life. She found that the only common connection between these kids was "grit" – the ability to continue despite discomfort or strain. When we allow our children to struggle, we covertly say to them that they are capable of succeeding without our help, and we allow them to build confidence (developed only through grappling with something hard/stressful and making it through). Allowing trials in your child's life isn't a sign that you don't care about them – it's a sign that you care so much about them that you are willing to make yourself very uncomfortable in order for them to experience better long-term outcomes!

Learning to tolerate distress isn't easy, and typically requires both practice and an understanding that being uncomfortable doesn't mean your child is doing things wrong….it means they are doing things right! Just as great exercise workouts result in sore muscles now but strength in the long term, being pushed slightly out of their comfort zone is necessary to help them develop resolve in times of distress,

The distress must be manageable! If the child is unable to manage the next step due to overwhelming distress, you may need to reconsider and adjust the level of difficulty. The benefit of building "challenge pathways" for our children is that they help us to think about and create a manageable step-wise approach to conquering difficult challenges by taking one small step at a time (especially if your child is able to help lay out the path!). We will provide more insight into challenge pathways in Chapters 5 and 7.

over the long term. Both parents and children benefit from understanding that in order to grow and get stronger and braver, discomfort is absolutely essential.

> Although we are suggesting that it is essential to "push" your child out of their comfort zone, be conscious of how often they are being challenged. If a child is constantly feeling "on the spot," they may feel taxed and less likely to "rise to the occasion." Some children may require a more nuanced and slower-paced approach.

You may be reading this and thinking that this all sounds great in theory, but how will I accomplish this? On the one hand, I'm being asked to challenge my child, but on the other hand, I'm being told that I should only push them slightly out of their comfort zone. What does this mean? How will I know when and how hard to push? The answers aren't always easy and you may not always know the right answer. We hope to help you find some answers in the next several chapters as we apply these theories to intervention specifically for SM. For now, we provide some broad and basic concepts to give you a better idea of what may be required:

* Learn to manage your own discomfort while watching your child struggle
* Understand that there will be occasional failures
* Trust that most children (yours included) can actually move more quickly in facing their fears than we imagine that they can
* Provide your child with controlled experiences and practical scenarios where they can practice being brave (be creative!)
* Help your child understand WHY you are asking them to feel uncomfortable (teach them about grit!)

Consider adopting a mantra to silently repeat when your child becomes upset, distressed, or otherwise melting down. It can be helpful and calming for parents to think and silently repeat something like, "I'm doing what's best for my child, I'm doing what's best for child" or "He will be ok, He will be ok" or "This work isn't easy but it's important!"

Preparing Your Child

Discussing selective mutism

Tears stained Jessica's pillow. "Mom, I tried to talk to my friend in class today, but the words just got stuck! Now she must think I'm such a snob. She looked really upset and just walked away when I wouldn't answer her. What's wrong with me?"

Explaining weaknesses and challenges to your child is no easy feat. It is difficult to strike a balance between confidence-building, hope-inducing, developmentally appropriate and empathetic descriptions of selective mutism. There are many ways in which SM could be explained to a child; some involve using the words "selective mutism," while others simply use descriptors of the symptoms.

Tips for discussing SM with your child:

* Start small and at an age appropriate developmental level. Younger children may need to understand very little about the process, except that we are practicing being brave when it is hard to get the words out. Older

children can understand more, but may need that information to come in small increments.

- Talk to your child when both of you are calm, and not immediately following an anxiety-provoking experience.
- Take care to talk with your child when you have their undivided attention (when you have them trapped in a car, they are a captive audience!).
- Normalize that everyone (adults, too!) has skills or behaviors that don't come easily for them. Give examples of other children who struggle with fears, weaknesses, or anxieties. You may even want to share some appropriate fears or worries of your own.
- Empathize with your child and tell them you understand that they try, but have a hard time speaking to people outside of the home. These people do not get to see your child as the wonderful, smart, awesome person that you are blessed to know.
- Give an age-appropriate description of anxiety and how it can cause us to avoid situations that are fearful. Depending on the age of your child, you can talk about the amygdala's role in anxiety and how this affects our body (fight, flight, or freeze response).
- Talk about the benefits of repeated practice. These practices are very uncomfortable at first, and are certainly not easy, but when we do them over and over they can become less difficult and more comfortable. It may help to think of examples where your child learned something after a lot of practice like riding a bike, playing a new instrument, or learning an academic subject. Remind your child that they are not alone and that they have a whole team working to support them.
- Convey the importance of becoming comfortable with the feeling of discomfort. When we feel this type of discomfort it means we are getting stronger and braver! It means that we are pushing ourselves past our comfort zone, or what is easy for us, and this effort is specifically what makes us grow!
- Assure them that you are there to help support them, and discuss possible reinforcements for hard work (e.g., privileges or rewards the child can earn) as well as the intrinsic benefits of speaking (e.g., being able to ask for help at school, making and keeping friends and showing how smart they are).
- End on a positive note of love and hope.

As parents, you know your child best, including which information will be the most meaningful and what they will be likely to understand. For a younger child, the conversation should be shorter, and should highlight that you understand it is sometimes hard for them to talk to people, but you will be helping them learn to be brave and strong. It might be hard at first, but as they practice it will get easier. Parents might wish to use toys or puppets in these explanations.

Older children may be better suited for a longer explanation. For example, a conversation may sound like this:

Jessica, I know we have talked several times about how hard it is to get the words out at school. Lots of kids have things they struggle with like learning to read, doing math, or climbing the rock wall at school. You are fantastic at those things, but I know when you try to talk it feels frustrating because it is very hard and makes you uncomfortable. Do you remember how we talked to Dr. Smith last week and played at her office? She has given us some information to help explain why it's a challenge for you to speak in school. There is a part of our brain that acts as a guard dog – it tells us when we should be scared and when we are okay. Sometimes we have a really good guard dog, the kind that knows when someone really dangerous is coming to our door. At other times, our guard dog is like a yappy puppy – it barks at everything! It barks at the postman, neighbors on walks, and even squirrels! It's so hard to tell when we should be scared or uncomfortable, because it's constantly barking at the wrong times! Dr. Smith explained that your brain might be doing that – passing on the message that things are going to be scary, hard, or uncomfortable too frequently.

Here is the great news – we can train our guard dog to do a better job. We can ignore him when he is over-reacting to the danger of a situation, and we can choose to act brave even when we don't feel brave! Practicing things that are challenging is the way we learn to do anything new. Do you remember when you first learned to do gymnastics? You could do cartwheels and handstands, but the idea of doing those on the balance beam was really scary! At first, you just didn't want to do it, and you tried to stay away from the beam. You even cried a few times when it was your turn. With help, you started doing small things on the balance beam to get comfortable. As you got better, you tried harder and harder moves. It wasn't easy, and occasionally it was scary, but every time you did it you got better and became braver. Now you don't even really think about it when you do your beam routine!

Using your voice at school is just like that. You will have a brave coach – someone who helps you know what moves to do, tells you how quickly to try the next move, and supports you while you learn. Your job is to work really hard, and to try to be brave even when you are scared or uncomfortable. In fact, that is exactly what brave is – doing something even though you feel scared or uncomfortable! You can't be brave without feeling scared! I know that this won't always be easy, so dad and I came up with some really cool prizes you can earn for brave work including TV time, extra time on your tablet, and some toys I know you really want. It will also be nice to eventually use your brave voice because you will be able to talk to your friends at school and have fun on the playground with them.

I'm really excited to work on this together as a team! You are such a smart, brave girl and I know you are going to be fabulous. I love you very much and I'm so proud of you.

If you do not feel as though you are capable of this conversation without help, a therapist or an understanding friend may be able to assist you in preparing for this discussion. You may also wish to have the therapist help you to deliver this message at your child's next therapy appointment.

To give the child a more tangible example of how anxiety goes away with practice, you might bring along a sour candy. When we first put sour candy in our mouth, it is very uncomfortable! It tastes terrible, and we want very badly to spit it out! Yet we keep it in and keep sucking on it, and just when we feel like we can't suck on it any longer, it starts to get easier. Our mouth gets used to the sour taste and stops telling us that this experience is awful and uncomfortable. In order to get to the sweeter flavor, we had to keep working through the discomfort. When we look back it seems manageable, and most of us would agree that we would be more confident to try sour candy again in the future. In fact, if we continued eating sour candies, eventually we would stop registering the sour taste.

It's not uncommon for kids to protest during this talk, making statements about how they can't do it, they aren't scared but instead just don't *want* to talk, don't care about prizes, etc. They may even become tearful. Be careful not to get into a debate. You are not trying to convince them of the plan or their diagnosis. Simply acknowledge their feelings ("This feels like it will be really hard" or "You aren't sure you are ready to do this hard work") and then move on.

When explaining SM to kids, it's probably best NOT to use the term "shy." Shyness is a temperamental characteristic and suggests that the child is always inhibited and quiet. For many kids with SM, this simply isn't the case. While they may be quiet and inhibited in school, they can be outgoing, loud, assertive, and they like to have fun in comfortable settings. Instead, describe the difficulty they have when using their voice with some people or talking in large groups.

Recognizing and Managing Discomfort

Be comfortable with discomfort!

Beyond educating your child on what SM is and how it works, it is typically beneficial to teach the child stress management techniques. While research suggests that the most helpful component of behavioral treatment for SM is exposure therapy (also referred to as brave practice), it is generally beneficial for children to have some calming strategies to use in the midst of anxiety-provoking situations.

Have you ever seen an Olympic swimmer before a meet? They stretch their muscles, take deep breaths, visualize the pool, and prepare themselves physically and mentally for the race. They understand that although they feel anxious and nervous, they can take charge of the anxiety so that it doesn't ruin their performance. First, they begin using a calm breath. They slow down their breathing, let their shoulders fall down away from their ears, and try to relax their muscles. They focus on slowly breathing in so that their stomach blows up like a balloon, and breathing out so that their balloon deflates. This is called diaphragmatic breathing, and research shows it reduces muscle tension and heart rate, allows mental function to slow and relax, improves concentration, and boosts confidence (Mayo Clinic Staff, 2011).

Next, tensing and relaxing muscles is helpful in releasing muscle tension. Many of us do this when we stretch in the morning – we tense our muscles as groups or an entire body, and then release. The release feels good and allows us to experience the looseness of muscle relaxation. There are many good audio tracks for children on progressive muscle relaxation including <u>I Can Relax!</u> by Donna

B. Pincus. Furthermore, there are apps for relaxation such as Pacifica™, Belly Bio™, Mindshift™, and Smiling Mind™.

Finally, parents and professionals can help children understand anxiety and the tricks it can play on us. When our yappy guard dog is barking, it is hard to tell the difference between real danger and a false alarm. Yet that is what anxiety usually is – a false alarm. If we can begin to understand and even predict when or where our brain will send us a false alarm, we can be prepared and simply work through it.

For example, if you were at work, and at 2 pm suddenly all the fire alarms began going off, you would likely rocket up in fear, grab your belongings quickly, and get out of the building! You would believe that you were in danger, and you would act on that potential danger. However, let's say that your boss came in that morning and told you there would be a test of the fire alarm system at 2 pm. You should stay at your desk and continue to work; they are just making sure the emergency system is in full working order. At 2 pm, when the system goes off, you will have predicted the sound and will continue to work, despite the discomfort of the alarm. You knew it was coming, and you knew it was a false alarm that provided no useful information. If we can prepare children with this same knowledge about their own brain and body, then when the alarms go off they can be confident in their ability to ignore the false warnings.

Finally, teaching kids to rate how *hard* situations or brave practices might be can provide valuable information and a way to communicate about their worries. Talk to your child about the difference between easy, medium, and hard brave work. Provide a visual rating scale (1 to 5 for younger children, 1 to 10 for older children) and describe how the different ratings might feel. Visual rating scales are easy to find on the internet, and you can tailor the one you use to your individual child - search "child SUD scale" (which stands for child subjective units of distress scale). Then, either provide example situations to the child and ask them to rate the difficulty, or ask the child to give you examples of what would be a 1, 5, or 10 on their scale. Asking the child what is scary, fearful, or worrisome is not as effective as asking them how "hard" a situation would be, as many children with SM do not self-identify speaking as "scary."

It is helpful to provide children with coping statements for times when the "fire alarm" is blaring but there is no danger including, "I can do this even when it's hard," "I can act brave even when I'm scared," "I'm not going to let these worries stop me," or "I've done really hard things before because I'm strong and brave."

Anxiety Rating Scale

This handout may be used with your child to rate the difficulty level of engaging; (1) with people - *the audience*, (2) in different places - *the environment*, and (3) with the type of speaking - *the speech demand*. The child might be instructed to think about (1) Who is it easy/hard to speak with? (2) Where is it easy/hard to speak? (3) What kind of speaking is easy/hard? Each column is independent and parents are encouraged to help the child fill in the blanks by providing them with examples (e.g. Where would grandma be on this sheet? What about the doctor? How hard is it to speak at church/school/baseball? Is whispering easier than speaking in full volume?) and also encourage the child to think of possible entries (e.g. Who else might be a 3? Where would speaking be a 5?)

Very EASY **1**	The Audience	The Environment	The Speech Demand
EASY **2**	The Audience	The Environment	The Speech Demand
FAIR **3**	The Audience	The Environment	The Speech Demand
HARD **4**	The Audience	The Environment	The Speech Demand
Very HARD **5**	The Audience	The Environment	The Speech Demand

One strategy for both increasing the likelihood of brave work completion, as well as helping add a twist of fun and excitement to the brave work, is including a simple reward system (Pinterest has thousands of ideas!). The main components of a great reward system include:

- ❖ **Goal behaviors:** What behavior do you want to see increase?
- ❖ **Tokens:** Items that signify movement toward rewards such as stickers, poker chips, points, etc. Tokens should be paired with verbal praise when praise is well-tolerated.
- ❖ **Rewards:** Rewards might include larger prizes that have to be earned over several work sessions like smaller dollar store gifts, treats, access to TV/ computer/tablet, privileges, extra time with parents, etc.
- ❖ **Creativity and consistency:** Even the best reward system can get old - parents should be creative, regularly add to the reward list, and be consistent about "paying out" when the child earns a reward or privilege.
- ❖ **A great tracking sheet of accomplishments**: Parents are encouraged to add stickers, notes, or decals to the Victory Valley worksheet when an important brave step is taken. It is rewarding for children to see their accomplishments and be reminded of the wonderful things they are achieving!

Beware possible errors in reward systems! These include not paying out for prizes when earned, inconsistency, lack of change to reward systems over time, giving up too early on reward systems, being unclear about the goal behavior, or prizes/ privileges that aren't truly motivating for a child.

Some parents are concerned about reward systems and feel that they are "bribing" the child for speech. Bribing is very different from rewarding; bribing is defined as giving a prize first in order to provoke the behavior (e.g., a child tells the parent that if they have a hamster, they will talk to their teacher, so the parent buys the child a hamster to evoke speech). Bribery generally occurs in distress; the parent is feeling upset and hopeless and is willing to do or give the child anything in order for them to be successful. Rewards are clear outcomes for appropriate or positive behavior. They are thoughtful and tied directly to a prosocial behavior. Reward systems are particularly useful because they result in repeated practice of a challenging behavior, and as the child practices repeatedly, they become more comfortable with the discomfort of speech. Furthermore, there is evidence that reward systems increase self-esteem, encourage children to make progress toward a goal, and make challenges more enjoyable.

Reward systems work for children of all ages. Young children will need very specific goals with quick "payouts" – an instantaneous return on investment. Thus, keeping small dollar store prizes, candy, or stickers on hand allow children to feel immediate pride. Tracking larger goals for young children can be done (in conjunction with an immediate reward) on a clear and fun handout or poster. For example, when a young child responds to her dance teacher's forced-choice question (goal behavior), they can get an immediate M&M, as well as a sticker on a "Brave Chart" working toward a larger prize.

Getting creative with rewards may be helpful or even necessary for kids who have very limited (or very expensive) interests; for instance, a unique reward may be getting to play the Pie In the Face™ game with a parent or a therapist.

Race Car Rally Reward Tracking
Use this worksheet to help your child track small steps toward reaching a goal.

Create Your Own Challenge, Design Your Own Reward
Use this handout to motivate your child to work toward and conquer a larger challenge.

Money Motivator Reward Tracking
This reward tracking worksheet is most appropriate for children who are learning the value of money or for those who understand the value of money.

Weekly Goals
This worksheet may be used at school, daycare, home, etc. It may be most impactful when used in the school setting, allowing teachers to track progress toward "brave" goals and communicate with parents.

Each challenge pathway conquered (or a difficult step accomplished) is an opportunity to claim a victory! Don't forget to help your child keep track of their victories on the Victory Valley worksheet if they find it motivating (chapter 7).

Older children and teens can understand the idea of "saving" toward a slightly larger reward. This can be tracked using anything convenient to the parents and engaging to the child, including marbles in a jar, checkmarks on a chart, points, "brave bucks" or poker chips. Older children may still enjoy tangible prizes, but many tweens and teens prefer earning privileges such as screen time, fun family activities, later bed time, movies, use of the phone, or special time with mom or dad. Parents should make these prizes or privileges within reach; making a goal too big (e.g., 100 points) may result in a child giving up before reaching the end.

The key to a good reward system is making it engaging (fun, bright charts) and reinforcing (prizes or privileges MUST be something your child wants or looks forward to). These plans need to be explained to the child so that they understand what behavior they need to do and what they can earn by doing it. Each time they meet the goal behavior, they should be reminded of what they did and what they earned (*"You answered the question from your teacher with your brave voice – great job. You earned a point, and now you have 4 points. You only need 2 more before you earn a family movie night – keep working hard!"*).

Parents can give out extra tokens for brave behavior outside of the specific goal behavior if the child has gone above and beyond expectations. It is important that tokens are not taken away for bad behavior, failure to meet a specified goal, or any other reason. Once the child has earned a token, it is theirs to keep, no matter how they do on future challenges.

Some children will begin to ask for rewards. If the child seems to be providing a simple reminder of brave work completed or if they are able to initiate their request to a new communication partner (such as their therapist), we would likely choose to comply with their request. On the other hand, some children will refuse to do brave work unless they are reinforced with rewards, and this is not a situation parents want to promote. Ideally, rewards encourage bravery, but with time and practice, rewards should be less necessary because there is less anxiety associated with the task. Eventually, an external reward will not be necessary because the child will feel an internal reward - the feeling of accomplishment that comes with positive social interactions.

Tracking, goal setting, and development of reinforcement systems can be tricky, especially for children who are very "stuck" in their anxiety. We always encourage parents and schools to reach out to mental health professionals with SM expertise when struggling to set up or perfect a reward system.

Keeping Organized

For some of us, keeping organized and staying on top of all the "to-dos" and paperwork can feel overwhelming. Consider a binder or digital filing system with clearly marked folders to help keep everything in one place and easily accessible. The example system below provides a way of organizing documents and information that might be helpful.

Notes Folder

Make notes, keep a log of progress and challenges:

- Interactions that are notable
- Brave work
- Successes/challenges at school, with family, friends, at church, in therapy, etc.

Medical/Therapy/Insurance Folder

- Insurance benefits information
- Names, addresses, contact info for service providers
- Paperwork from office visits
- Test Results
- Payment information & progress toward deductible

Planning & Worksheets Folder

Keep a record of the hard work that your child has completed and plans for the future!

- Worksheets & planning sheets from this book
- Your child's psychologist, school counselor, speech therapist, etc. may provide worksheets as well

School Folder

- Special Education Plans (IEP, 504, accommodations, etc.)
- Communications with teachers, admin and staff
- Progress reports, report cards and state testing results
- School work examples

Research Folder

As you begin to research SM, place materials in this folder so they will be available when needed:

- Notes on treatment options, books, topics that you've researched or have an interest in researching
- Medical research

Miscellaneous Folder

- If it doesn't fit any where else, put it here!

We have accomplished a lot while traversing the Foundational Foothills and preparing for the rest of the journey ahead – we've learned about the people who can help guide us, and how to prepare ourselves, our team, and our child for a successful intervention. We've taken time to review and become familiar with Mount Mindful and many of the skills that will help children be more mindful and aware during the intervention. In the next chapter we provide the tools that will help your child progress through the main domains of Peers Peak, Community Crest, and School Summit to find their brave voice. Learning how to use these tools flexibly will help you craft an individualized plan with unique challenge pathways to help your child overcome selective mutism!

Selective Mutism
An Overview for Treating Professionals

What is selective mutism (SM)?

Selective mutism is a childhood anxiety disorder characterized by a child's inability to speak and communicate effectively in **select** social situations, such as school. Children with SM are able to speak and communicate in situations where they are comfortable, secure, and relaxed (usually with their family at home).

SM is **NOT** normal shyness, stubbornness, or deliberate defiance. It is currently understood as a type of social anxiety and children with SM may have a fear of others hearing their voice.

Key Behavioral Indicators

- Ability to speak normally with some people, but may use a whisper or modified voice, provide only a very short response, or may not speak at all.
- "Blank" or "expressionless" face when speech is expected.
- Avoids eye contact.
- Awkward/stiff body language
- May communicate nonverbally - nodding, pointing, and even smiling but they will not speak.

SM impacts each child very differently, however some common impacts include:

- Difficulty speaking in the school environment
- Situational avoidance in speaking with neighbors, unfamiliar adults & children, and even some relatives outside of the immediate family
- Struggling to speak in environments and with people where there is a history of avoidance
- Difficulty in starting new activities and meeting new people

Learn more about Selective Mutism:

selectivemutism.org
childmind.org
selectivemutismlearning.org

When does SM usually begin and how long will it last?

SM is typically noticed at the start of daycare, preschool or kindergarten but many caregivers observe signs and symptoms earlier. For the majority of children with SM, intervention will be necessary in the form of exposure based behavioral therapy with a therapist. Children who do not receive effective treatment may continue to struggle with SM into the elementary, middle and in some cases, high school years.

Why do children develop SM?

SM is generally understood to have genetic, biological, environmental and temperamental components. It is **NOT** caused by trauma, abuse, or bad parenting.

Ideal treatment for children with SM:

- Exposure based behavioral therapy with a therapist (preferably with experience or willing to learn and consult with an SM expert)
- Parent training and school support so that parents and the school become comfortable with and part of the intervention team
- Gradual exposure to situations where the child is able to take small steps to conquering challenges (e.g. speaking with teachers, ordering food, etc.)
- Medical intervention with SSRI when necessary

Diagnostic Codes for Selective Mutism

SM is considered an anxiety disorder and is coded for billing purposes as *313.23 (F94.0)*.

I am Brave

Instructions: Fill in the blanks below to recall ways in which you've been brave!

ONE List three ways in which you have been brave.

TWO List three things you've learned that were hard at first but now seem easier (e.g. swimming, tying your shoes, learning to add double digits, etc.)

THREE How do you feel when it's hard to speak in some situations?

FOUR How do you feel a when you are brave by conquering a new challenge or speaking? Do you feel excited? Happy? Relieved?

FIVE How might you feel if you could speak every time you need to speak?

SIX Think of five positive things that have happened because you were willing to try something hard. (e.g. getting to swim in the deep end, making the math team, having a sleepover, etc.)

Race Car Rally

Instructions: Check off each triangle flag on the roadway (or place a sticker over the flag) and write down each positive step toward reaching a goal in the table below.

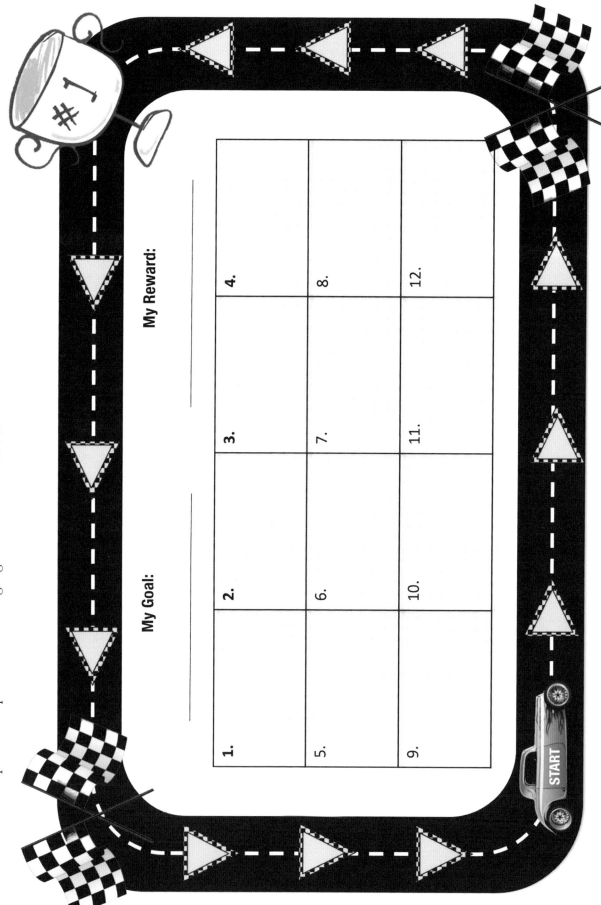

My Goal: _____   **My Reward:** _____

1.	2.	3.	4.
5.	6.	7.	8.
9.	10.	11.	12.

Create Your Own Challenge *Example*
Design Your Own Reward!

Instructions: Use the spaces below to document ten instances of brave work. If you choose, small items or privileges may add up to a larger reward (use the space on the bottom to create a list). Allow your child to draw a picture of their reward or document their feelings below.

Brave Work Practice: *Gesturing, giving and taking*

1	6/7/18 : At the store, she handed the cashier a credit card and took the bag	**6**	6/14/18: Smiled at the mail carrier and took the mail
2	6/8/18 : She took a cookie from our neighbor and looked up at her	**7**	6/15/18: Handed the library card to the librarian and shook her head no when the librarian asked, "Have you read this book?"
3	6/9/18: She smiled at the usher and handed him the tickets	**8**	6/17/18: At the store, handed money to cashier and received the change
4	6/10/18: Shook her head yes at the dry cleaners when asked if is she was going swimming!	**9**	6/18/18: At the sandwich shop, pointed to the toppings she wanted and smiled
5	6/12/18: On our walk, a neighbor stopped us and she didn't look down! She even smiled a little when the neighbor said, "See you later."	**10**	6/19/18: Waved goodbye to a family friend!

Draw your reward (or feelings) here:

Special day with mommy

If applicable, write down and check off small items or privileges here:

On my day with mommy:

- ☑ *Donut for breakfast*
- ☑ *Special TV time*
- ☑ *Go to nail salon*
- ☑ *Pizza for lunch*
- ☑ *Go to a movie*
- ☑ *Candy at movie*
- ☑ *Make a craft*
- ☑ *Extra IPAD time*
- ☑ *Ice cream after dinner*
- ☑ *Stay up late*

Create Your Own Challenge

Design Your Own Reward!

Instructions: Use the spaces below to document ten instances of brave work. If you choose, small items or privileges may add up to a larger reward (use the space on the bottom to create a list). Allow your child to draw a picture of their reward or document their feelings below.

Brave Work Practice:

1		**6**	
2		**7**	
3		**8**	
4		**9**	
5		**10**	

Draw your reward (or feelings) here:

If applicable, write down and check off small items or privileges here:

Money Motivator Reward Tracking

This reward system can be used in conjunction with any challenge your child is working to overcome. Just add check marks each time "money" is earned in the appropriate bubble. At the end of each week or when you decide the "challenge" is over, help your child to calculate the money value of the marks they earned. If you choose, use the worksheet on the following page to record weekly totals toward a specific larger reward. This system works best for older children.

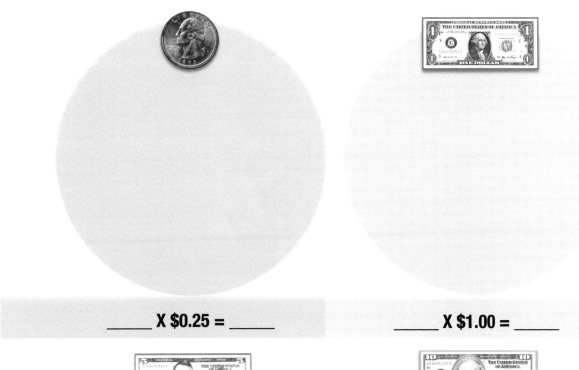

_____ X $0.25 = _____   _____ X $1.00 = _____

_____ X $5.00 = _____   _____ X $10.00 = _____

	Q	$1	$5	$10	
TOTALS:	_____ +	_____ +	_____ +	_____ =	_____

Money Motivator Reward Tracking
Totals Sheets

I need to earn: $ _____ **to buy:** _____

Date	Dollars	Current Total	Notes

Weekly Goals

BRAVE GOALS

Week of _____

	Monday	Tuesday	Wednesday	Thursday	Friday
1.					
2.					
3.					
4.					
5.					

Comments:

Conceptualization of Selective Mutism

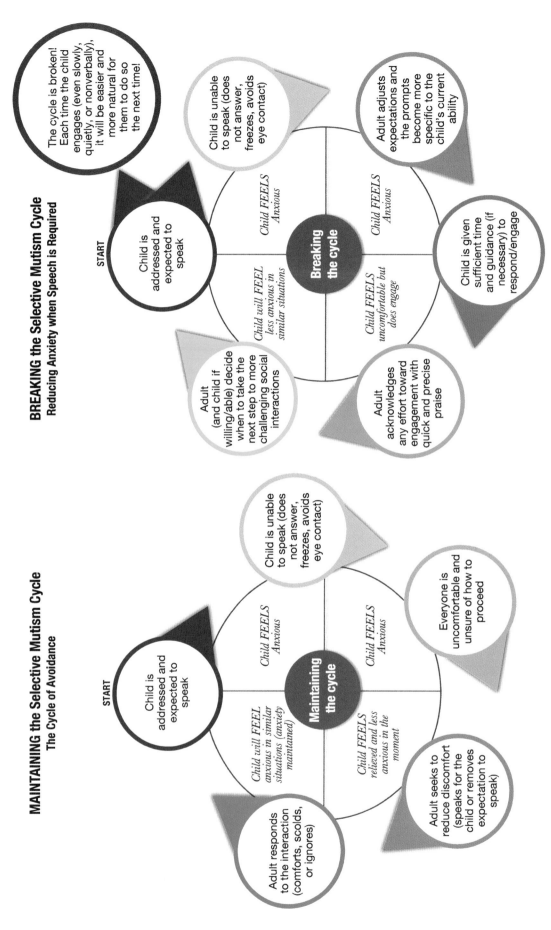

MAINTAINING the Selective Mutism Cycle
The Cycle of Avoidance

START

Child is addressed and expected to speak

Child FEELS Anxious

Child is unable to speak (does not answer, freezes, avoids eye contact)

Child FEELS Anxious

Everyone is uncomfortable and unsure of how to proceed

Maintaining the cycle

Child FEELS relieved and less anxious in the moment

Adult seeks to reduce discomfort (speaks for the child or removes expectation to speak)

Child will FEEL anxious in similar situations (anxiety maintained)

Adult responds to the interaction (comforts, scolds, or ignores)

BREAKING the Selective Mutism Cycle
Reducing Anxiety when Speech is Required

The cycle is broken! Each time the child engages (even slowly, quietly, or nonverbally), it will be easier and more natural for them to do so the next time!

START

Child is addressed and expected to speak

Child FEELS Anxious

Child is unable to speak (does not answer, freezes, avoids eye contact)

Child FEELS Anxious

Adult adjusts expectations and the prompts become more specific to the child's current ability

Breaking the cycle

Child FEELS uncomfortable but does engage

Child is given sufficient time and guidance (if necessary) to respond/engage

Child will FEEL less anxious in similar situations

Adult acknowledges any effort toward engagement with quick and precise praise

Adult (and child if willing/able) decide when to take the next step to more challenging social interactions

It is completely natural (and even socially expected) to "help" a young child when we see them struggle. Parents and other "rescuers" are not to blame - we do NOT cause the presentation of SM although we may contribute to the maintenance cycle. We need to re-learn what it means to "help" so that we can help in a different way - breaking the cycle! Think about the people who rescue your child. It might be worth sharing an explanation of the cycles with these individuals (in an age appropriate manner).

Chapter Five

INTERVENTION TOOLS FOR COMMUNICATION SUCCESS!

Understanding the Toolkit

Tools for overcoming selective mutism

The wonderful thing about trying to overcome selective mutism now vs. twenty years ago is our recent advancements in the understanding of SM and the "tools" available for treatment. In this chapter, we will introduce these tools and we will revisit them in Chapter 7 to explain how to use them flexibly. If one tool "fails" or doesn't seem to be working optimally, another is likely available to meet the intended goal. Some challenges might even require using a combination of tools. We recommend that parents become familiar with each tool we describe in this chapter so that if it is needed, it will be accessible!

> *We become what we behold.*
> *We shape our tools and then our tools shape us.*
> **—Marshall Mcluhan**

Tools for Communication Success
Specific strategies used to promote speech

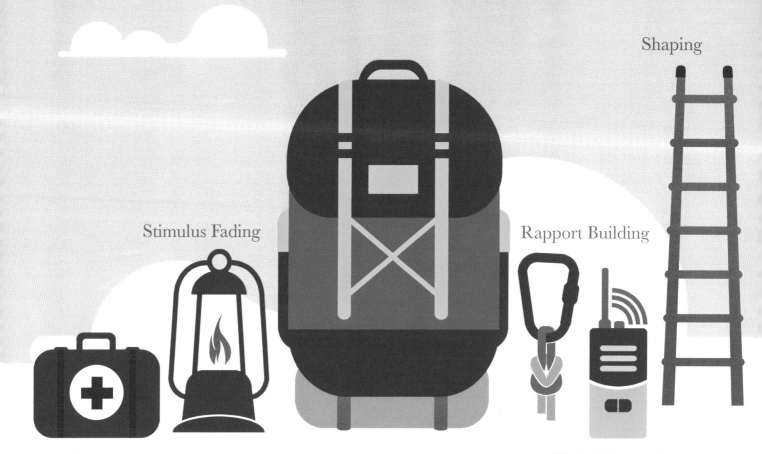

Shaping

Stimulus Fading

Rapport Building

Medical Intervention

Verbal Prompting

Rapport Building	A specific and planned approach to providing a comfortable environment and building trust, to set the tone for a positive interaction
Verbal Prompting	Providing specific and targeted prompts, directing the child in a way that optimizes their ability to respond
Stimulus Fading	The process of taking existing speech and adding in new communication partners slowly or moving the speech into new environments
Speech Shaping	The prompting and practicing of slow steady steps toward increasingly difficult levels of speech
Medical Intervention	Selective Serotonin Reuptake Inhibitors (SSRIs) may be prescribed for children who are struggling to participate in behavioral therapy and make progress toward overcoming SM

Tool #1 Rapport Building
Child Directed Interaction

Child Directed Interaction (CDI) is a specific rapport building intervention that not only promotes a positive relationship with the child (a necessity of any good therapeutic intervention) but also sets the stage for the brave work that will come later (Carpenter, Puliafico, Kurtz, Pincus, & Comer, 2014). While there are many helpful ways of building rapport, CDI is a structured model (from Parent/Child Interaction Therapy, or PCIT; McNeil & Hembree-Kigin, 2010). In addition to building rapport, CDI skills can be used to help a child warm up (e.g., at the start of the school day), calm down when they are overwhelmed, and to generally help them feel positive and understood.

If a therapist is working with your child using Child Directed Interaction, you can expect:

If your child is specific about the toys they enjoy playing with or if they are showing a keen interest in a special toy at the time of your appointment, bring it along!

- **The therapist will engage in one-on-one play with your child in a private setting (perhaps with you present).**
  This will allow the therapist to focus on the child and remove any possible barriers to the child feeling comfortable and relaxed.
- **The therapist will play at your child's developmental level and follow their lead.**
  Activities that lend themselves well to this type of play include open-ended, creative play such as arts and crafts, constructional toys such as Legos, building blocks, magnetic blocks, dollhouses with miniature people, and marble run sets. With older children, developmentally-appropriate (e.g., more complex) arts and crafts projects, board games, apps, etc. can be used to interact. It is helpful to let the therapist know what your child enjoys playing with and/or what might interest them.
- **The therapist will use PRIDE skills to build rapport.**
  PRIDE skills are rapport-building techniques designed to encourage positive interactions and enhance relationships. As the child begins to reach a comfort level with the therapist, the therapist may direct the parent to slowly disengage and perhaps leave the room.

Parents are oftentimes directed to use CDI skills with their children prior to intervention at a therapist's office or prior to embarking on brave practices with their children in the community.

PRIDE skills are the most dependable way to quickly build rapport
with children and may be used by parents, family members, friends,
therapists, coaches and teachers!

Child Directed Interaction
Pride Skills for the child with SM

		Examples	Purpose
	**PRAISE** Appropriate Behavior	❖ Terrific counting! ❖ Thanks for letting me know. ❖ You have wonderful ideas for this game. ❖ I love how you used your brave voice.	Praising makes both the adult and child feel good, adding warmth to the relationship, while letting the child know what the adult likes. Praise leads to increased self-esteem and positive behavior choices.
	REFLECT Speech & Non-Verbal Communication (if it occurs)	Child: I made a star. Adult: Yes, you made a star. Child: (*Points at a dog picture*) Adult: You want me to see the dog picture. Thanks for showing me!	Reflections slowly begin to desensitize the child to the fact that the adult hears what they are saying. They also increase the child's verbal communication and improve speech.
	IMITATE Appropriate Play	Child: I am putting baby to bed. Adult: I will put sister to bed too. Child: (*Draws a sun in the sky*) Adult: I am going to put a sun in my picture too.	Imitating the child's play allows them to lead the interaction and it also validates their play choice; they feel empowered when the adult chooses to follow along.
	**DESCRIBE** Appropriate Behavior	❖ You are making a tall tower. ❖ You drew a smiling face. ❖ The cowboy looks happy. ❖ You are putting that together so well. ❖ You chose the red marker.	Describing the child's actions helps to hold their attention and shows the child that the adult is interested while also modeling appropriate speech.
	**ENTHUSIASM** (Subtle, reserved)	❖ Wow. ❖ That's great. ❖ That is super. ❖ I love building blocks. ❖ (*Smiling*)	Showing enthusiasm will provide the child with a sense that the adult is interested, having fun and enjoying the interaction, which strengthens the positive relationship. Take care not to overwhelm the child with too much enthusiasm.

Don't give Commands	Don't ask Questions	Don't correct or Criticize
Will not allow the child to lead, resulting in a hierarchical relationship ❖ Hand me that paper. ❖ Tell me what letter this is. ❖ Make the sun yellow and the sky blue. ❖ Go grab that toy over there.	May reinforce avoidance by increasing the child's anxiety (the time for questions is later, after rapport building) ❖ That is a blue one, right? ❖ What shape is this? ❖ Are you drawing a castle? ❖ Do you want to play with the blocks now?	Creates an unpleasant interaction, one that does not build rapport and may possibly lower the child's self-esteem ❖ Don't scribble on your paper. ❖ You've put that piece in the wrong spot. ❖ You are being difficult. ❖ Don't touch that.

Verbal Directed Interaction (VDI) (Carpenter, Puliafico, Kurtz, Pincus, & Comer, 2014) provides the structure and framework for successful verbal prompts. It provides a flowchart of how to prompt, how to react to speech, and what to do when the child doesn't respond (Kurtz S. , 2017). The adult is tasked with changing the way in which children are prompted to speak or engage. We can think of VDI as a verbal "sleight of hand" - it happens without the child realizing it's happening, but remarkably the changes in the way we address and interact with the child can make all the difference. Typically, these strategies are used in the context of stimulus fading and shaping (see Tools #3 and #4) and occur after the adult has built rapport with CDI.

First, the child is prompted to speak with a forced-choice or open-ended question. For children who are just beginning to speak comfortably, forced-choice questions provide a great structure for a response, as they give the child the correct response options and they need only choose one and say it (examples of these types of questions can be found on the *Helping a Child to Respond* handout). This type of question bypasses any processing or language issues they might have and prevents the child from freezing due to anxiety about the "right" answer. Children with no speech issues, or those who are milder in their presentation or further along in treatment, may benefit from a mix of forced-choice and open-ended questions. Avoid yes/no questions, if possible, as they allow (and even encourage) head nodding and shaking. Remember, VDI emphasizes verbal communication as compared to CDI where nonverbal responses are acceptable.

After asking the question, the adult waits at least 5 (painful!) seconds. If the child responds verbally, the adult gives calm labeled praise and a reflection of what the child said ("You want a brownie - thanks for letting me know," "Brownie - great answer," or "I love that idea – I love brownies").

If the child responds nonverbally (shrugging shoulders, pointing, nodding), the adult acknowledges the gesture but prompts again for a verbal response ("I see you nodding, but I'm not sure which one you were nodding for…Do you want a brownie or a cookie?"). If the child responds, calm praise and reflection are given.

If the child does not respond, wait five seconds and re-ask the question (make sure you have formatted the question as forced-choice, and that the question is clear and easy to answer; if not, this is a great point at which to reformat your question). If the child responds, give calm praise and reflection. If the child does not respond, make the prompt easier. Ways to make the prompt easier include pulling the child aside in a private area, requesting the first sound of the word, returning to a previous question the child was able to respond to, or reminding them of possible rewards for using their brave voice.

Helling a Child to Respond
Using Verbal Directed Interaction for SM

When should I use Verbal Directed Interaction (VDI)?

At the doctor, grocery store, library, or anytime that your child is prompted to speak but seems unable to do so!

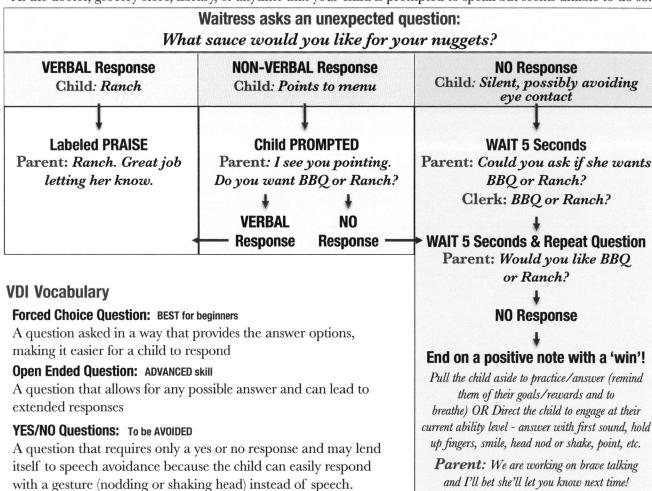

Waitress asks an unexpected question:
What sauce would you like for your nuggets?

VERBAL Response	NON-VERBAL Response	NO Response
Child: *Ranch*	Child: *Points to menu*	Child: *Silent, possibly avoiding eye contact*
Labeled PRAISE Parent: *Ranch. Great job letting her know.*	**Child PROMPTED** Parent: *I see you pointing. Do you want BBQ or Ranch?*	**WAIT 5 Seconds** Parent: *Could you ask if she wants BBQ or Ranch?* Clerk: *BBQ or Ranch?*
	VERBAL Response ⟶ **NO** Response ⟶	**WAIT 5 Seconds & Repeat Question** Parent: *Would you like BBQ or Ranch?*
		NO Response
		End on a positive note with a 'win'! *Pull the child aside to practice/answer (remind them of their goals/rewards and to breathe) OR Direct the child to engage at their current ability level - answer with first sound, hold up fingers, smile, head nod or shake, point, etc.* **Parent:** *We are working on brave talking and I'll bet she'll let you know next time!*

VDI Vocabulary

Forced Choice Question: BEST for beginners

A question asked in a way that provides the answer options, making it easier for a child to respond

Open Ended Question: ADVANCED skill

A question that allows for any possible answer and can lead to extended responses

YES/NO Questions: To be AVOIDED

A question that requires only a yes or no response and may lend itself to speech avoidance because the child can easily respond with a gesture (nodding or shaking head) instead of speech.

VDI Practice: Modifying Prompts

YES/NO Questions	Forced Choice Questions	Open-Ended Questions	Open-Ended Follow-up
Do you like dogs?	Do you like dogs or cats better?	What is your favorite animal?	Why do you like dogs?
Are you in science class this year?	Do you have biology, chemistry, or neither this year?	What science class are you in this year?	What is your project for the science fair?
Do you want a sandwich for lunch?	Would you prefer a sandwich, hot dog or something else?	What do you want for lunch today?	What are some of the things you like to eat on hot dogs?
Do you want to play with the blocks?	Do you want to play blocks, the puzzles, or something else?	What do you want to play with?	What are some of the things you like to build with blocks?
Is your birthday in June?	Is your birthday in June or July?	When is your birthday?	What will you do for your birthday?
Did you travel on a plane?			
Can I open your juice box?			

With VDI, we suggest that you avoid the following scenarios:

- ❄ **Don't accept a nonverbal response such as shrugging or nodding:**
  Unless this is the current step on the pathway, it does not promote growth; instead, pull the child aside where they may be more comfortable verbalizing or make the response easier.

- ❄ **Don't move on without waiting at least five seconds for an answer:**
  Some children will need additional processing time; give them time to muster the courage!

- ❄ **Don't forget to praise or reflect the child's response:**
  By doing so, you are letting them know that they have been heard. Some children need to know that their efforts are appreciated.

- ❄ **Don't pepper the child with too many questions:**
  Children need time to respond, so peppering them with questions at "rapid fire" may cause them to feel overwhelmed and to shut down.

- ❄ **Don't ask very difficult or complex questions:**
  If we set the bar too high, they won't be able to reach for it! These questions should not be testing the child's knowledge or speech capabilities; they should only be challenging the child to speak.

- ❄ **Don't give over-the-top, excited praise:**
  If we become too animated and excited, many children will feel embarrassed. We must be mindful that some children do not want attention to be drawn to them.

Tool #3 – Stimulus Fading

Transitioning communication to a new audience or environment

Certain people and environments are especially challenging for children with SM. Stimulus fading is a fancy label for the slow and thoughtful transition of a new communication partner into existing speech or moving speech from a location where the child speaks to a location where the child currently does not speak. Instead of a new person abruptly approaching your child in the midst of their anxiety and asking a pointed question, fading allows the child time to "desensitize," or get used to, the new communication partner through slow, measured steps. We offer a common but basic handout about stimulus fading on the next page to point out just how "slow" you may have to proceed in order to desensitize a child. We review three other common scenarios in more detail later in this section: helping children transition to speech with a new communication partner, helping children transition to speech within a small group, and helping children transition to speech in a new location.

Stimulus fading tends to be the most direct, easiest, and most generalizable intervention to use, so it's a very important tool for your toolbox! However, it

Adding New Communication Partners
Using Stimulus Fading with CDI & VDI

What is stimulus fading for selective mutism?

Stimulus fading is a behavioral intervention technique used to take the existing speech of a child and expand (generalize) it to new people, places, or activities.

Why is stimulus fading effective?

Stimulus fading provides for small steps and the slow introduction of new communication partners while children interact playfully with a parent or comfortable communication partner.

How is speech elicited with the stimulus fading technique?

The child should be engaged in fun, familiar, simple speech demands - board games that promote speech, naming or counting activities, scripted pretend play (e.g. school, restaurant, etc.) and reading aloud.

Where should stimulus fading take place?

Until a child is comfortable speaking with a new communication partner, stimulus fading should take place in a private setting, such as an office, empty classroom, or the child's home.

Who should be involved?

A comfortable communication partner, such as a parent or therapist, should engage the child in play and elicit speech while a new person slowly enters the interaction.

Example Scenario:

1
Child warms up in room, speaking with their parent or a comfortable communication partner.
Parent and child play in a room, using games that naturally elicit speech.

2
Child speaks in vicinity of new person.
New person enters room (but does not pay attention to the child) and the child continues speaking to parent.

3
New person attends to the child's speech.
New person looks at child, nods, laughs, or smiles in response to what the child says.

4
New person acknowledges the child's speech through reflection.
"You want to play with the dolls next - great idea!".

5
New person asks questions to the child and the child answers.
"Are you going to play with the boy or the girl dolls?"

6
Parent fades out of the interaction, leaving child to speak independently with the new communication partner.
Mother leaves to use the phone, and the child continues to answer the new person.

requires one thing – existing speech that another person could overhear. If your child is unable to speak at all in the proximity of another person, or speaks only in a very quiet whisper directly in your ear, using stimulus fading may not be possible at the moment. To determine whether to use stimulus fading, ask yourself these questions:

- ☀ Does the child speak to me in the environment where we will be practicing (e.g., school, grandma's house, playground)?
- ☀ If someone enters slowly, is it likely that the child will continue speaking to me in a volume that others might be able to hear?
- ☀ Do I have access to a private location in that environment (e.g., a private room in the school, a very quiet corner in the gymnastics class, a study room in the library)?

If your answer is yes to all questions, stimulus fading is likely the best place to start. Stimulus fading should be thought of as slowly bringing someone new into a conversation or verbal exchange *or* moving speech to a new location and can be done in several different ways. Here are some general examples using the stimulus fading tool (but stimulus fading can be used in a multitude of different ways, so we encourage you to be creative!):

Parents should carefully determine appropriate adults for stimulus fading. Important caregivers, teachers, and adults who have adequate time and commitment to the child can make excellent new communication partners. However, parents should also consider that some adults may be "contaminated." Occasionally, novel or less familiar adults are easier for the child to speak with initially.

Speaking with a Teacher for the First Time
Stimulus Fading Example

The goal is to get the teacher, a new communication partner (NCP), into the room, with the child continuing to use appropriate speech. A parent, the current communication partner (CCP), is tasked with keeping the child speaking with fun activities that encourage speech, using forced-choice and open-ended questions. In the example below, we guide you through a stimulus fading procedure with the goal of a child speaking with a teacher for the first time. **The parent will be the CCP and the teacher will be the NCP.**

1. The parent and the child should have some time to "warm up" in the room, playing and talking alone with the door almost closed. During this time, full speech or a loud whisper (not a quiet whisper) must be obtained consistently before a new individual begins fading in. Don't forget that using CDI skills is a structured way to help your child speak and feel confident during this time. (*If several sessions pass and the child cannot warm up to the point of consistent speech, intervention must shift to shaping; see tool #4).

Parents should be sure to keep up a consistent but natural rate of questions/conversation through fun, engaging play.

2. The teacher begins fading (or entering) into the room when the parent has obtained an appropriate volume of consistent speech from the child. The teacher should **NOT** respond in any way to what the child says or act as if they are attending to the child at this time. The teacher should very slowly enter the room, as far away from the child as possible, and busy themselves (i.e., type on the computer, pick up the room, or do paperwork). If the child discontinues speaking or shows other signs of anxiety, slow the entrance even more or stay in the same position for several minutes until it appears that the child's anxiety is reduced and speech resumes.

3. The teacher should slowly start making their way toward the child by finding activities to do in closer proximity to the interaction but should continue to pay no overt attention to the child. Movement should continue to occur (slowly) if the child is still responding consistently to the parent.

4. When the teacher is close to the interaction and the child is maintaining speech, the teacher can begin to silently attend to the interaction (e.g., occasionally looking up at what the parent and child are doing, laughing when something funny occurs, smiling and showing enjoyment). No questions or comments should be made at this time.

Parents who would like video examples of stimulus fading are encouraged to watch the "SM Mock Fade-In Procedure" video on the Thriving Minds Behavioral Health YouTube channel, or the "Understanding and Managing Selective Mutism" video on the AnxietyBC YouTube channel.

5. If the child tolerates attention to their speech, the teacher can begin to reflect or respond to what the child is saying. For example, if the child tells the parent that they picked an elephant, the teacher could reflect, "Oh, you picked an elephant." If the child tells the parent that he played his new videogame last night, the teacher could comment, "You played your new game – that sounds like fun." Again, **NO** questions should be asked at this time.

6. When this seems comfortable and minimally anxiety-provoking, the teacher can begin asking occasional forced-choice questions.
    a. Follow the VDI flowchart (Tool #2).
    b. If the teacher needs help finding the right time to ask a question or using the forced choice format, the parent could suggest a question (e.g., "Mrs.

Smith, I can't tell if she picked a bird or a butterfly. Can you ask her if she's got a bird or butterfly this time?").

c. If the child finds it too challenging to respond directly to the teacher at first, Plan B (or making it easier) might include the parent repeating the question, and when the child responds, the teacher will reflect by saying "Thanks for telling me."

7. When the child is consistently responding to the teacher, the parent can begin to slowly fade out of the interaction and then the room, leaving the teacher and the child to continue interacting independently. Be sure to leave the room very slowly and naturally as this fading out process should never feel abrupt (e.g., check text messages or emails on your phone, stretch your legs by walking around the space, look at artwork on the wall, etc.).

If the teacher is unable to complete all steps in one session, at the next opportunity for a stimulus fading procedure the teacher could start outside the room again but attempt to fade in more quickly. This does not have to be the same day but should be as soon as possible (preferably within a few days).

If at any point the child stops speaking, the parent should make every attempt (through prompting, distraction, and reward systems) to re-engage the child in speaking. The teacher should stop and stay where they are. Sometimes, it is helpful for the teacher to take away any attention or even turn their body away from the child. A last recourse would be for the teacher to leave the room, let the parent re-establish speech, and then slowly return. Any loss of verbalizations should be considered a red flag for the teacher to move more slowly next time.

Speaking with a Small Group of Peers

Stimulus Fading Example

Once a child has been successful in adding communication partners privately, or if the child already speaks to many people one-on-one and struggles instead to speak to groups, the next step should include fading into a small group. In the example below, the child can speak in one-on-one situations but struggles to speak during small group activities.

1. A comfortable adult, one with whom your child currently speaks (usually a parent, teacher, keyworker, or therapist), should start engaging the child in an activity that requires or prompts for speech, preferably something the child finds enjoyable (board games, telling jokes, reading aloud, playing Twenty Questions, etc.). A small peer group should be generally out of earshot, engaging in a separate activity (e.g., playing a game themselves). They should be

instructed before intervention to continue playing the game and not to attend to the other game (the child with SM or the adult working with them) until they are prompted to play.

2. As the child with SM gets comfortable speaking, the adult and child should slowly move toward the peer group (while maintaining speech). As they move closer to the group, the child's anxiety will likely increase initially, but will decrease with time.

3. When the child with SM and the adult are close to the peer group, and the child is still speaking to the adult, the peer group should be instructed to watch but NOT to comment or ask questions about the game that the adult and child are playing (e.g., "Hey, guys – I don't know if you know how to play this game that James and I are playing? Why don't you watch us quietly for a few minutes so you can learn but please remain quiet and don't ask any questions until I tell you that it's okay.").

Be aware of Pathway Hazards - Only change one factor at a time (audience, environment, speech demand); if you are working to obtain speech in a new environment, the audience and the speech demand (or activity) should remain the same. For example, the adult should work independently with the child in a new environment before attempting to introduce new speaking partners in that same context.

If the child stops speaking as they near the peer group, the adult should move physically back to the last spot where speech was consistent with the child, and try to re-establish speech (e.g., "Oh, let's move back to the wall and start our game again"). This may be an indication that either the child is not quite ready to be introduced to a group of peers or the child needs to be moved more slowly toward the group.

4. Assuming that the child with SM maintains speech with the adult while the peer group is observing, the adult should engage the peer group in playing the same game (so that the child isn't speaking directly to the peer group members, per se, but is engaging verbally in the game with them).

5. After the child is speaking in front of the peer group, as part of the game, the adult may wish to directly prompt the peer group members to ask questions of the child (e.g., "Brandon, ask James if he wants to play this game again or a different one").

6. Finally, if the child is maintaining speech within the peer group, and the peer group members are engaging the child with SM as they would other peer group members (not avoiding asking questions or leaving the child out), the adult can begin fading out of the game. First, they might disengage attention from the game, then move away, before finally leaving the interaction altogether.

Speaking in a New Location

Stimulus Fading Example

Some children are very restrictive about the environments in which they will speak. For example, they might be used to speaking in the therapist's office, but as soon as the door opens, they become mute. Others might talk all the way to school, but as soon as the car is parked on school grounds, they shut down. For these children, stimulus fading of environments may be helpful.

1. A comfortable adult, one with whom your child currently speaks (usually a parent, teacher, keyworker, or therapist), should start engaging the child in an activity that requires or prompts for speech, preferably something the child finds enjoyable (board games, telling jokes, reading aloud, playing Twenty Questions, etc.). This interaction should begin in an environment where the child is already used to speaking comfortably.

2. Once the child is speaking consistently in the comfortable setting, the interaction should slowly move to a new environment. Each step should be slow, and the adult should wait for the child's anxiety to increase and then decrease before more movement is attempted. For instance, while playing a speaking game like Headbanz™ or a fun speaking app on the phone, the adult might first open the office door, then move toward the doorway, slowly out in the hall, and finally walk down the hall. It is important to maintain speech throughout the movements; if speech is lost, the adult should cue the child to move back to the location where they were last speaking comfortably, prompt again for speech using a game or activity, and then move forward more slowly.

If your child questions why the activity is moving to a new environment, games that require movement can be helpful in transitioning the activity to a new environment in a more natural way such as a bean bag toss, I Spy, etc.

Tool #4 – Shaping

Helping the child with SM take small steps toward speech

Stimulus fading (Tool #3) is considered the go-to intervention for children with SM because it is often successful. However, for some children it is not possible to use stimulus fading in the beginning of the intervention. The child may completely shut down near a new communication partner, or parents/caregivers may not be able to attend school to help with stimulus fading exercises. Peers may be hard to fade in due to young age and inability to follow directions. In these cases, shaping might be a better tool to try.

Where stimulus fading is taking pre-existing speech to a new environment and with new people, shaping is taking small but mighty steps to increase speech complexity while keeping all other factors (environment and audience) the same, beginning at the child's current ability level. Some children may be able to consistently use gestures to convey information; if so, that should be the beginning point. Others may be able to make sounds but not speak; if so, that should be the beginning point. Many children enjoy beginning with blowing air, as this is fun, interesting, and seems to have very little (in their mind) to do with speaking. As the child becomes more confident with one step, a new step can be added and practiced. Once the child becomes verbal consistently, the goals can increase to not only encouraging more/longer speech, but to taking this new speech and switching to stimulus fading (tool #3) to add in more conversational partners and environments.

There are countless ways to help shape speech. You will find ideas and activities on the next page to get started. This is not an exhaustive list; be creative! Also, don't be afraid to add small steps between the examples below if the child seems to struggle.

The journey of a thousand miles begins with one step.

–Lao Tzu

A Step-Wise Approach to Confident Conversation
Shaping Speech

Starting & maintaining conversations
Scripted -> prompted -> spontaneous speech, socials stories and social skills books (e.g. Jed Baker books), role playing (starting, maintaining, exiting social interactions), professional interview practice

Initiating Speech
20 questions, knock knock jokes, telling a story or acting out a story, person bingo, interviews (child -> you, you -> child), requesting help, Show & Tell™ game, Puppet Pals™ App, Headbanz™, requesting help, take turns asking questions, Toontastic™ app, story starter cards, Heads Up™ app

Speaking multiple word responses & longer utterances
Telephone game, reading, songs, TV jingles, "Tell me about…", role playing, "What's Wrong" pictures, finish the story, barrier games, carrier phrases, sequencing stories

Speaking one word responses (e.g. answering forced choice questions)
Board games, making choices, fill in the blank, complete the sentence, Sparklefish™ app, Super Duper™ app, Go Fish!™, Hangman™, Old Maid™, Battleship™, Smarty Ears™ app, hot/cold game, making choices in play, what's missing games, Uno™, counting tasks, Akinator™ app, Mad Libs™ app

Combining sounds to make words
Shaping discrete sounds into sound combinations to make words, begin with Yes/No: Y+ES = Yes, N+O = No, other examples: H+I = Hi, M+E = Me, R+E+D = Red, GR+E+N = Green

Making voiced sounds and/or animal & environmental sounds
Making animal sounds in response to a picture of an animal, making letter sounds from flash cards, making first sounds from Uno™ cards, tongue clicking

Making voiceless sounds (s, t, p, k, h, f, sh, ch, voiceless th)
Snake sound, cotton-ball races with sounds, flat tire sound, pinwheel with sounds, identifying sounds in magnetic letters

Blowing air
Cotton-ball races, bubbles, balloons, pinwheels, straw painting, blowing tissues, Free Candle™ app, Bubblegum Hero™ app

Making faces without the use of the mouth
Mirrored faces, silly faces, feeling faces, oral-motor exercises, Funny Faces™ game

Making noise without the use of the mouth
Clapping, stomping, snapping, musical instruments that do not require the mouth (e.g. drums, tambourine, cymbals, etc.), rain sound, tapping foot to the music

Using gestures (writing, pointing, nodding/shaking head, shrugging shoulders, etc.)
Charades, songs with hand movements (e.g. Itsy Bitsy Spider), thumbs up/thumbs down, practice giving and taking things from NCPs, Where's Waldo™ books, I spy, picture exchange cards, yes/no questions, Kids on Stage™, interview game (with yes/no questions), Pictureka ™, making choices

Following directions of a new communication partner (NCP)
Simon Says, arts & crafts, board games, cooking, attaching a direction to a high-likelihood activity, dot-to-dot, barrier activities, classroom helper, red light/green light, scavenger hunts, sorting tasks

Medication can be a very helpful tool in the treatment of selective mutism. Selective Serotonin Reuptake Inhibitors, or SSRIs, are the most commonly used medical interventions for SM due to their success and research basis in treating other anxiety and mood disorders. The most commonly used and studied medications for treating SM are Sertraline (Zoloft) and Fluoxetine (Prozac), likely because of their historic use in treating social phobia and the low occurrence of negative side effects in children (Barterian, et al., 2018).

Medication is best used *in addition* to appropriate behavioral treatment. Consider the scenario of learning to swim. Children are not born knowing how to swim, so parents provide life jackets. However, it is not long before the life jacket becomes constricting (it rescues and accommodates!) – it doesn't allow children the independence to learn how to swim. Thus, parents switch at some point to water wings or some other method of flotation support to help keep their children afloat (but not hinder learning) as they begin to swim.

Medication is often used in a similar manner – it supports children, keeps them "afloat," and reduces some of the struggle in order for them to focus on brave work and building brave muscles. Eventually, we hope that we can reduce or remove medication after the child has built brave muscles and sufficiently practiced the brave work. Many experts in the field of SM highlight that this period of time on medication is likely more than a year since it can take several months to get to a correct, sufficient, maximized dose of medication followed by time for the child to practice brave work and build up self-confidence.

A large, multi-site research study called the Child/Adolescent Anxiety Multimodal Study (CAMS) compared the effectiveness of cognitive behavioral therapy, Zoloft, and the combination of both against a placebo for the treatment of anxiety in children and adolescents. According to the CAMS study (Compton, et al., 2010), 81% of children made positive and notable improvements when receiving cognitive behavioral therapy and Zoloft, whereas only 60% made gains with CBT alone and 55% with Zoloft alone. The study was conducted on

Child & Adolescent Anxiety Multimodal Study (CAMS)

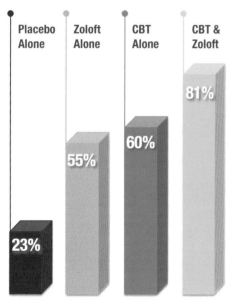

Percentage of children making positive & notable improvements

The National Institute of Mental Health Study of separation anxiety disorder, generalized anxiety disorder, and social phobia in 488 children with an average age of 10 to 11 years. The study compared cognitive behavioral therapy (CBT) alone, medication alone, placebo, and combined medication and CBT.

❖ *NO DIFFERENCE in overall rates of side effects among groups - SSRIs were deemed safe.*

❖ *> 80% of responders maintained gains at 34-36 weeks*

children with an average age of 10 to 11 diagnosed with a wide range of anxiety disorders including social phobia.

This data suggests that approximately 60% of kids with anxiety benefit from cognitive behavioral therapy alone. That is an encouraging statistic and it means that many kids may not need to take medicine to make progress. Cognitive behavioral therapy is not recommended for children until approximately age 6 to 9 because they do not have the cognitive skills necessary to participate (e.g., awareness of their own thoughtss, perceptions, and internal world). For young children with selective mutism, exposure-based behavioral therapy is the gold standard. When children are not demonstrating significant progress through exposure-based therapy, parents and clinicians must determine if medication might be helpful. It can be controversial to put young children on medication and some parents are strictly opposed to doing so. Many parents carefully weigh the pros and cons to make a decision. Doctors will typically begin considering medicine based on the following criteria:

- ❂ Children who have had a poor response to behavioral therapy (see Parent Pointer)
- ❂ Selective mutism symptoms are moderate to severe (significantly impairing the child's functioning)
- ❂ A family history of an anxiety disorder or SM
- ❂ Children with coexisting psychiatric problems such as social anxiety disorder, separation anxiety, or generalized anxiety disorder.

If you feel as though medication might be right for your child, consider the following:

- ❂ Some primary care physicians and pediatricians are willing to prescribe SSRI medication to treat SM, while others prefer to refer out to psychiatrists (physicians with expertise in the pharmacological treatment of mental health issues).
- ❂ SSRIs are typically prescribed at a low dose initially, and then increased slowly, with the physician keeping a close eye on side effects and effectiveness.
- ❂ Because it takes several weeks for the medication to build up in the body, no or only minimal changes may be seen for the first few weeks. Around approximately two weeks, many families report some minor changes occurring, and maximal changes on that dose will be seen in approximately four weeks.
- ❂ Depending on the outcome of the low dose that was first administered, the physician may increase the dose to help support maximal changes.

Determining when medication is appropriate for your child may be a difficult consideration for both you and your child's physician. Physicians generally follow a set of guidelines/criteria when considering medication; however, some of the criteria are subjective. It may be difficult to know at what point behavioral therapy is not working effectively, or whether your child falls into the category of "more severely impaired." They will rely on your reporting and perhaps the suggestion of your child's therapist. As a parent, you might consider the quality of treatment that your child received (e.g., was the therapist informed and experienced with treating SM?), how your child responded to treatment, and what other options are available to help your child make progress (e.g., Is it feasible to work with a SM expert?).

If you feel like you are "spinning your wheels" with no progress, it might be time to consult with a physician and review your child's history to determine if it's the right time to try medication.

Common concerns regarding medication:

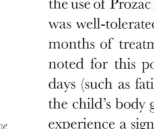

Other alternative pharmaceutical and homeopathic treatments considered by parents may include essential oils, CBD oil, diet changes, and acupuncture; however, these interventions have not been fully evaluated for effectiveness and safety in children and should be considered with care in conjunction with consultation from your child's pediatrician.

1. **What will the side effects be?** A few research studies specifically focus on the use of Prozac in young children with SM. These studies indicate that Prozac was well-tolerated and safe for children over the course of approximately six months of treatment (Dummit et. al., 1996). The most common side effects noted for this population are general physical complaints for the first few days (such as fatigue and upset stomach), though these typically go away as the child's body gets used to the medication. Additionally, some children can experience a significant disinhibiting (or agitation) effect, where they become very active, irritable, and have a hard time sleeping. Again, this typically only lasts for a few days, but should be reported to the prescribing physician if it occurs.

2. **Will my child become addicted? Will they always have to use medication?** These are two very different questions, but are often asked together. SSRIs are not addictive so there is no risk of a child (or adult) becoming addicted to them. It is impossible to estimate how long a child will need to take medication. Some children can take the medication for one year, receive excellent therapy and treatment, and begin to wean off the medication successfully. Other children will need medication long-term to help control anxiety. It is always the decision of the parent whether to begin and continue treatment with medication; you are not committing your child to a life of medication use by attempting a trial of medication now.

3. **They are just fine at home, so why should I medicate them for something that doesn't happen all of the time?** Many parents feel that if the child only struggles at school and in public, this doesn't constitute enough of a reason to use medication. However, parents must remember that important responsibilities and opportunities in a child's life occur in the school and in extracurricular or social settings. Without every opportunity to be successful in these areas, a child may fall behind in school, have difficulty developing and maintaining friendships, and become less confident. Some anecdotal evidence suggests that kids who are untreated or not adequately treated may develop depression or other anxiety disorders, and might self-medicate in the future.

4. **Will this make them suicidal?** Many parents have heard of the "black box warning," or the labeled warning on SSRI boxes following a public report by the FDA about the increased risk of suicidal thoughts in teens with depression who were taking SSRIs. It is important to note that this warning refers to teens with depression (not anxiety) and the research study on which the black box warning was based found only some increase in thoughts of suicide, not actual

attempts. This effect has not been reported in anxious children, including those with SM (Food and Drug Administration , 2016).

How will I use these tools in "real life"?

It's time to grab your imaginary backpack filled with all of our tools for overcoming selective mutism as we journey on to illustrate ways in which these tools can be used successfully and flexibly within the school and in the community. We ask that you "carry" (or understand) all of these tools so that if you need them, you will have them. Every child will respond differently to intervention, so utilizing tools that match the needs of your child is paramount. Keep in mind, too, that while one tool may work well in the beginning, you may need to shift and use a different tool to keep progressing along the pathway toward confident conversation.

A Step-Wise Approach to Confident Conversation
Shaping Speech

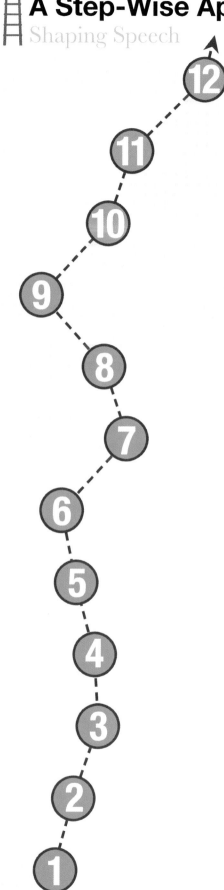

Chapter Six

EDUCATION PLANNING: WHAT YOU NEED TO KNOW TO SUPPORT YOUR CHILD AT SCHOOL

Many children with selective mutism experience significant anxiety throughout their regular school day. They fear being called on, they may feel like they are the center of attention at all times, and they worry about what people would say, do, or expect of them if they do talk. Since this fear in the school setting impacts so much of the child's day, it is vital to begin the process of planning appropriate interventions and accommodations with your child's school.

Depending upon the age of your child, the assistance that they need will vary. Children are typically identified or diagnosed with selective mutism between the ages of 6 and 8, putting them in early elementary school (and a large majority of those children will be in the public education setting). In this chapter, we focus on education planning for the elementary years but we do recognize and highlight the impacts of helpful accommodations for SM during the preschool years as well as the middle/high school years.

Common Impacts of Selective Mutism in the School Setting

Preschool	Elementary School	Middle/High School
☀ Difficulty or inability to respond to the teacher in the classroom, and therefore struggles with group activities, circle time, show and tell, and verbal assessments ☀ Difficulty requesting to use the bathroom ☀ Difficulty eating lunch when others are present	☀ All impacts listed for preschool ☀ Inability to ask clarifying questions or request help from the teacher ☀ Difficulty or inaccuracy in the academic assessment process ☀ Difficulty or inability to benefit from social learning opportunities ☀ Difficulty or inability to engage the help of others when necessary for educational, health or safety reasons ☀ Inappropriate behaviors or feelings under normal circumstances ☀ Difficulty or inability to participate in group work or group projects	☀ All of the impacts listed for elementary school ☀ Difficulty or inability to participate in oral presentations ☀ Difficulty making and keeping friends ☀ Inability to learn through repetition of concepts by teaching others ☀ Inability or difficulty completing independent, age appropriate tasks (e.g. driving, pumping gas, etc.)

*We outline the basic steps, but for more detailed information we recommend parents visit the Wright's Law website at **wrightslaw.com**– it is filled with extensive detail about the process and what to expect.*

Given the significant impacts that SM may have on a child's social and academic functioning in the school setting, many children will need accommodations, assistance or special education services in the school setting to ensure they meet their greatest potential.

The chart on the next page, *Establishing an Education Plan for your Child*, provides an eight step process to help navigate a public education system full of unspoken rules and steps that are not always obvious to parents. Navigating the education system is probably more of an art than a science.

1 Understand Options for Accommodations and Special Education

Every child in our country has the right to a free, appropriate public education (FAPE). When a child is unable (due to emotional, physical, social, or cognitive reasons) to obtain that free, appropriate education, accommodations and/or interventions should be provided to assist the child. This can be accomplished in three ways - Individualized Education Plans, Section 504 Plans, and unofficial accommodations. The path you take depends on your child's needs, the severity of their challenges, the school's resources, and the intervention team's recommendations.

Individualized Education Plan (IEP)

An IEP is a document that outlines the needs of the child, the services that will be provided to meet those needs in the school setting, and the goals that child is expected to meet over the course of the year. In order to qualify for an IEP, the child must meet certain criteria in different categories and their school performance must be impacted by the challenges that they face. Because an IEP is the only special education plan offering direct service with school support staff and is highly regulated, it is typically the plan that we recommend considering first. (It is important to note that private schools do not typically provide special education services or implement IEPs, so this may not be an option if your child is in a private school with no public funding).

> It is not enough to simply have a clinical diagnosis of a learning, behavioral, or emotional disorder – the school must also deem that the child's academics are adversely impacted by their symptoms in order to qualify for special education services.

In total, there are 13 categories under which a child could qualify for special education services. The three categories outlined below are the most commonly used for children with selective mutism:

Speech/Language Impairment (SLI) – defined as a communication disorder that adversely affects a child's learning. A language disorder "may be characterized by difficulty in understanding and producing language, including word meanings

Establishing an Education Plan for your Child

Understand the Options

More Formal Path Individualized Education Plan (IEP)		Less Formal Path 504 Plan or Accommodations
	Request Help from School 	
Formal written request for a comprehensive evaluation delivered to school		Informal request for a meeting with the teacher and/or other school personnel
	Determine Needs 	
IEP evaluation carried out by the school, including observation		Meet with teacher and other school personnel, share knowledge about SM, your child, and specific requests
	Eligibility Decided 	
If eligible, a meeting will be scheduled to develop an IEP. A 504 plan may be suggested if IEP is denied		School/teacher determines feasibility of requests and will either agree to or deny accommodations
	IEP Meeting/Write a Plan	
The IEP meeting will result in a customized IEP tailored to the needs of the child.		A 504 plan will be formalized (varies by district) or accommodations plan finalized
	Services/Accommodations Delivered	
Accommodations and services are delivered as mandated by the IEP		Accommodations are delivered as specified by a 504 plan or an accommodation plan
	Review Progress	
Progress should be reviewed as often as possible to ensure needs and goals are being met		Progress reviewed often to determine if a more formal plan is necessary to ensure needs are being met
	Re-evaluate Needs	
Goal-setting annually with a formal re-evaluation every three years required by law		An annual review of accommodations with a new teacher is suggested. Switch to formal path if necessary.

(semantics), the components of words (morphology), the components of sentences (syntax), or the conventions of conversation (pragmatics)" (Head Start, 2006). Children with selective mutism may have primary disabilities in speech (including semantics, articulation, and fluency), but they also have social pragmatic speech weaknesses (the ability to utilize speech effectively in social situations).

Other Health Impairment (OHI) – defined by IDEA as a chronic or acute health condition which limits alertness in the educational environment due to either limited strength, vitality, and alertness or heightened alertness to the surrounding environment; these must impair academic performance (Grice, 2002).

Emotional Disturbance/Disability (ED) – defined by IDEA as one or more of the following emotional or behavioral issues:

- ☀ An inability to learn that cannot be explained by intellectual, sensory, or health factors
- ☀ An inability to build or maintain satisfactory interpersonal relationships with peers and teachers
- ☀ Inappropriate types of behavior or feelings under normal circumstances
- ☀ A general pervasive mood of unhappiness or depression
- ☀ A tendency to develop physical symptoms or fears associated with personal or school problems

Many schools do not have extensive knowledge of SM, and therefore may not realize the adverse impacts that SM can have on learning. They may also be unaware that children with SM are often eligible for special education services with an IEP under one these three categories due to the significant adverse effects SM has on a child's social and academic functioning.

Section 504 Plan

If a child does not qualify for special education services or whose needs do not warrant individualized intervention in the school, such as one-on-one services, a Section 504 Plan might be considered to provide accommodations in the general education setting. A Section 504 Plan is not considered special education, but it is an "adaptations and modifications" plan specifically intended for the classroom setting (mandated by the civil rights law establishing the rights of individuals with disabilities). This document provides the child with in-classroom accommodations, but no direct, individualized services are inherently included (i.e., the child will not obtain one-on-one sessions). A Section 504 Plan may be an appropriate fit for students with mild to moderate SM who do not need specialized services but instead need minor accommodations for specific situations, such as oral presentations or participation points in the classroom setting. Later in this chapter, we provide a list of common accommodations provided to children with SM in the classroom.

IEP Category Request Form

This form outlines the three most common categories for which children with SM may be found eligible for special education services. The form can be provided to the school with the IEP request letter (also known as special education consideration) or it may be used to dispute the category your child has been assigned.

The graphic below is intended to highlight the differences between an IEP and a 504 Plan. Knowing the differences and understanding the process for obtaining these specialized education services is a great starting point and may help you feel more confident when requesting help from your child's school.

Key Differences between an IEP and a 504 Plan

	Individualized Education Plan (IEP)	504 Plan
Applicable Law:	Individuals with Disabilities Education Act (IDEA) Federal Education Special Education law for children with disabilities	Section 504 of the Rehabilitation Act of 1973 Anti-discrimination, civil rights statute to prohibit discrimination based upon disability
Eligibility Requirements:	❂ The child must meet one of 13 specific disabilities listed in IDEA. ❂ The disability must affect the child's educational performance and ability to learn.	❂ The child may have ANY impairment that substantially limits a basic life activity. ❂ The impairment must be documented.
Who Participates?	Strict legal requirements govern who must be present at meetings: ❂ Child's caregiver ❂ Child's teachers (at least 1) ❂ A spec. ed. teacher (at least 1) ❂ School Psychologist or Specialist ❂ A representative from the district's spec. ed. services	There are NO legal requirements governing who must be present for a 504 meeting but participants may include: ❂ Child's caregiver ❂ Child's teacher ❂ School counselor ❂ School administrator
Plans Include:	Every IEP must include specific information such as: ❂ Services to be provided ❂ Annual education goals ❂ Accommodations & modifications ❂ A plan for standardized testing	There are no specific standards for 504 Plans and they will vary widely but generally include: ❂ Accommodations to be provided ❂ A designated party responsible for overseeing the plan ❂ A designated duration (usually the school year)
Plan Management:	The IEP team reviews the plan at least once per year and a formal re-evaluation must be conducted every three years to determine continued eligibility.	The specifications for plan management vary by state and district but generally will include an annual review of accommodations to determine continued eligibility.

Requesting special education services for your child does NOT mean that you are asking for your child to be placed in a "self-contained" special education classroom. You are requesting services so that your child can remain in the general education setting.

Accommodations

If a child is attending a private school or has mild SM, an unofficial accommodation plan may be considered. Private schools are not legally mandated to provide special education services or even 504 Plans to students with disabilities but may (and should) still allow for accommodations within the classroom or even direct intervention in the school. This plan may have similar characteristics to an IEP or Section 504 Plan but does not have governmental oversight.

If a private school is not providing adequate services, switching to a public school may be considered as an avenue to obtain the services your child needs to succeed.

② Request Help from the School

Before sending your request letter to the school, make a copy for your own records.

Once you've determined the best path forward for help (IEP, 504 or unofficial accommodations), you must contact the school and request a meeting.

If you believe that your child might be eligible for special education services with an IEP, they must be "referred" (or brought to the attention of the special education team at the school). The most effective way to refer your child is to write a letter to the principal and special education administrator at the school (copy the teacher as well) outlining your concerns and requesting an evaluation for special education consideration. It is important that parents take this official route of requesting, in order to get the best and most efficient response from the school. We provide a sample IEP meeting request letter (also known as special education consideration) at the end of this chapter.

> To meet the requirements of consideration for a special education evaluation to obtain an IEP, a formal written request is necessary to ensure an evaluation will be scheduled. Having a note from a physician or psychologist stating a diagnosis or a need is not enough.

Your written request should include the date, the reasons for your concern, contact information, and if you are trying to bolster your effort, you might include the IEP category designation that you believe your child might best fit. By including the IEP category handout at the end of the chapter, you are providing the school team with the most common categories that are used to justify eligibility for children with SM and demonstrating that you are aware that other children with SM have qualified for special education services. Parents are encouraged to highlight their specific concerns, particularly the ways in which the child is impacted academically by selective mutism.

IEP Request Letter (also known as special education consideration)
An example letter to the school requesting an IEP or a Section 504 Plan. This form may be modified to request unofficial accommodations as well.

After receiving the letter, the school will schedule a multi-disciplinary meeting where the team will discuss which evaluations need to be completed in order to determine eligibility. It may be wise to contact the school district's special education department to inquire about the timeline for evaluation and determining eligibility as they can vary by state or district.

If you prefer a Section 504 Plan or an accommodation plan, generally a letter or phone call requesting a meeting with the school to discuss possible accommodations is sufficient but it certainly wouldn't hurt to submit the more formal written request.

③ Determine Needs

Next, the school will conduct an evaluation to determine if the child meets the criteria for special education or accommodations. Parents will be asked to provide consent for their child to be evaluated; the parent may request at that time to receive a list of tests, observations, or questionnaires that will be used during the evaluation process. For children with selective mutism, it is important that a few evaluative tools are used:

1. Appropriate questionnaires, including the Selective Mutism Questionnaire (Bergman, 2012) and general anxiety or emotional/behavioral questionnaires, such as the Multidimensional Anxiety Scale for Children (March, 1998) or Behavioral Assessment System for Children (Reynolds & Kamphaus, 2015)
2. An interview with parents to ascertain background information, including the speaking behavior of the child in school, in public, and in the home setting
3. An observation of the student in the classroom setting, in less structured academic settings (e.g., recess or lunch), and in performance-based settings (e.g., during a group project or when called upon by the teacher)
4. A video of the child speaking comfortably in the home setting, if possible
5. A speech evaluation (if indicated) examining both receptive and expressive communication

If the school is not using the right evaluative tools, you may request more appropriate tools to be included as part of the evaluation process.

If your child is currently seeing a therapist outside of the school or was evaluated by a therapist outside of the school system, provide their reports, or request a letter from the therapist detailing why the child meets the diagnosis of SM, what they are currently working on in treatment, and the specific recommendations the therapist might have for school intervention or goals. Parents are also allowed to invite outside therapists to meetings as support or another source of information. Schools are not bound to take all of the recommendations by an outside therapist, but they do have to consider them.

4 Eligibility Decided

The appropriateness and eligibility requirements for an IEP, Section 504 Plan or unofficial accommodations are different and each of these options has a distinct threshold for meeting requirements.

Just because your child doesn't have a formal IEP or 504 plan does NOT mean that you cannot schedule a meeting with the teacher, counselor, or a school administrator. Each new year is an opportunity to provide important information to your child's school/teacher so that they can better work with your child.

- **IEP** eligibility is determined by whether the child meets the definitions of IEP disability categories listed in IDEA. If the child's needs cannot be addressed through education in a general education classroom alone, and if these challenges impact educational performance, a child will be deemed eligible for services as outlined in their IEP.

- **Section 504 Plan** eligibility is determined by whether a child fits the Section 504 definition of a disability. Do they have a physical or mental impairment that substantially limits one or more major life activities? If the answer is yes, then the child will be deemed eligible for a 504 Plan to meet their specific needs (Wright & Wright, 2007).

If 30 days pass with no word from the school, do not hesitate to call the school, email, or send another letter as a reminder.

❖ **Unofficial Accommodation Plan** eligibility will be solely decided at the discretion of the school. The needs of the child will be considered and weighed against the school's ability to carry out the needed accommodations. The school may be more willing to help if they have sufficient resources available.

If your child is deemed eligible for an IEP with special education services, the school has 30 days to schedule a collaborative meeting to review your child's needs (the IEP Meeting) at a time that is convenient for the parents and the school team. If you have not done so already, you are advised to "align your ducks," in other words, make sure you are prepared and confident for the IEP meeting. Who will attend the meeting along with you, what resources and information will you need to bring, and what are the main intervention goals and accommodations that you wish to discuss on your child's behalf?

If an IEP is not deemed an appropriate fit for your child, the school team and parents should still convene to discuss the needs of the child and make a plan to assist him/her outside of the confines of an IEP. Perhaps a 504 Plan or accommodations might be a better fit.

⑤ IEP Meeting/Make a Plan

The IEP meeting (or a less formal meeting if an IEP isn't appropriate) is an opportunity to bring together your child's team of helpers and experts to plan possible interventions, accommodations, and to set goals that will ultimately lead to your child receiving the best educational experience possible. The meeting will include parents and your child's school team which might include the principal, teachers, interventionists (speech pathologist, social worker, school psychologist), and any outside counsel the parents wish to include. Outside counsel may include additional caregivers, advocates, or outside therapists. It is important that the interventions and the goals set are specifically designed to increase your child's confidence and bravery. It is essential that practices be designed to take place in a slow, stepwise manner. For instance, if a child is seeing a speech pathologist, they may eventually have a goal of working on articulation or pragmatics, but the first goal will generally be to increase speech. Goals should provide steps for moving systematically from avoidance or nonverbal responding to verbal responding, in a variety of contexts and with a variety of individuals.

*The **Getting to Know Me Form** with a photo of your child and the **Quick Tips for Successful Communication** handouts can be helpful for specials and substitute teachers who do not see your child every day. Consider requesting that these handouts be provided to substitute teachers.*

The following handouts are available at the end of this chapter. These handouts are helpful to provide to meeting attendees and can be used during planning meetings and beyond.

IEP Meeting Notes Template Meetings can be a whirlwind of information and oftentimes it can be difficult to recall details. We recommend using this template to take notes during IEP/planning meetings.

IEP Goal Planning Sheet & Example This document will assist you in helping to take a more active role in developing goals for your child's IEP. We recommend reviewing this form prior to the meeting and thinking about possible accommodations/services that may help your child. This form may be viewed as a working document during goal planning meetings. In addition to the blank form, we've included an example of a completed form.

Services / Accommodations Goal Tracking Form and Example

The blank version of this form may be used by service/accommodation providers to track your child's progress, to help you to verify that services are being regularly performed, and to note your child's progress toward their goals. Ultimately, for a child with SM, this means that service/accommodation providers are effectively moving your child toward increased speech across situations/people. In addition to the blank form, we've included an example.

Getting to Know Me Form and Example

This form includes a basic explanation of SM and space for you to provide specific information about your child and their strengths and weaknesses. Included is a blank form to be filled in by a parent/caregiver that can be shared with individuals working with your child and an example of a completed form.

Quick Tips for Successful Communication

With this document, we have attempted to create a one-page tip sheet to help engage children with SM in a way that will reduce anxiety and create a relaxed setting for speech to occur more naturally. It can be shared with all school personnel, even those who rarely come into contact with your child in the school setting.

If the parent/caregiver is able, and the school allows it, they may play an active part in helping their child overcome SM in the school setting, even acting as the keyworker. Some children will respond better and make progress more quickly when a parent/caregiver is present while other children will find it more difficult when a parent is involved. You should have a good sense for which of these scenarios will work best for your family.

   During the meeting, it is also important that the school identify the primary interventionist, or "keyworker." The keyworker is the individual in the school setting who will be responsible for the brave work intervention, data collection on progress, generalizing speech to other adults and peers, and communicating with parents, the outside psychologist (if there is one), and other school staff. In most scenarios, the keyworker is either the speech pathologist, school psychologist, social worker, or guidance counselor, because they have a background and/or training with children who have emotional needs (such as anxiety) or speech weaknesses. However, parents should also be open to others as keyworkers in the school setting if (1) the noted individuals do not have enough time to see the child with necessary frequency – we recommend 2 to 3 times per week for 15 to 30 minutes, (2) their personalities do not mesh well with the child's temperament, or (3) the noted staff members are not motivated to learn about or engage with a child with selective mutism. Good keyworkers may even include para-professionals, resource room teachers, special education teachers, school nurses, or parents. Because we recommend at least one hour of individualized intervention per week, we typically advise against the child's primary teacher taking on the role of keyworker. Teachers are so busy, they have so much to do in so little time, that we are wary of assigning them this additional responsibility.

At the end of the meeting, parents must be in agreement with services provided, service providers identified, and goals written in order for the intervention to begin. When parents are in agreement and sign the IEP document, the services and accommodations will begin immediately.

Bring treats to the meeting. No kidding - delicious treats will go a long way in creating a softer environment!

Don't forget to add all correspondence, forms, notes and handouts, from the meeting, to your binder or electronic filing system.

Services/ Accommodations Goal Tracking Form and Example

An example tracking form to verify that services are being regularly performed and are "successful" in making progress toward increased speech with new communication partners and in new locations.

A few Strong Recommendations for Meetings:

1. Be respectful and easy to work with. Parents must first advocate for their child's needs, but being perceived as a bully is rarely the best way to obtain services.
2. Take notes at all meetings and keep all correspondence with the school. Even if you have the kindest principal or special education director in the country, and they are happily providing your child with all the love, support, and intervention you request, they could be replaced with someone who is less inclined to provide services. At that point, you would need documentation. We provide several helpful sheets at the end of this chapter to help you stay organized during the IEP meeting and beyond.
3. When attending a meeting, it may be helpful to provide informational sheets on SM. We find that the conceptualization of selective mutism handout (Chapter 4) helps school personnel understand the cycle of avoidance and what they can do to help.
4. Provide a short informational sheet about your child's strengths and interests as well as information about their challenges and needs. Additionally, you may wish to provide a short fact sheet on how to best interact with your child to boost communication success. At the end of this chapter we provide a sample "Getting to Know Me" template and example. We also provide a sheet titled, "Quick Tips for Successful Communication".

6 Accommodations/Services Delivered

The goal of school intervention is to increase confidence and speech at school, so that the child is able to engage fully in the classroom (including responding and initiating to teachers and peers, answering questions, doing oral presentations, participating in group projects, etc.). In order for a child to progress along the path to communicating freely in the school setting, they may need special accommodations to coincide with the behavioral intervention "tools" that we discussed in the previous chapter. Regardless of the type of plan your child is participating in, the following accommodations might be considered. This is not an exhaustive list but rather a list of common and helpful accommodations. When determining accommodations for your child, consider those that provide the child with ways to access the full academic and social experience at school.

Common Accomodations for Children

- Allow child's parents/family members to have access to the school environment during off hours (before/after school, during summer months) to promote comfort and verbalization when alone with a parent and eventually, one or more peers or a teacher
- Early arrival to class for warm-up in the morning
- A bathroom buddy and scheduled times for restroom breaks
- Providing a nonverbal way for the child to indicate that they need to use the restroom, such as a card they flip over on their desk, or verbal prompts from the teacher to stop and use the restroom
- Alerting the child/parent to changes, such as a substitute teacher or a fire drill
- Extra time to respond and/or wait time for responses
- Interacting by asking choice questions rather than open-ended questions
- Communication cards (this should be considered short-term as to not provide an avoidance strategy)
- Reinforce/praise when child engages in appropriate social interactions (privately if child doesn't like attention)
- Social stories to increase confidence in how to engage in social interactions
- Role-playing opportunities for more anxiety-provoking occurrences (e.g., show and tell or class presentations)
- Introduction to potential teachers (for the following year) in the spring before school is dismissed
- Visit to the new classroom prior to the start of the year, at least one week before the start of school
- Child should be encouraged to increase communication/participation in the classroom and in social interactions (even if that communication is nonverbal at first). Eventually, attempts should be made to reinforce and attend to only verbal language, so as to extinguish the use of nonverbal communication.
- Information on the student's needs will be conveyed to substitute teachers

Elementary School

- All or some of the example services listed above for preschool
- All adults who come into contact with the child should be advised of the intervention plan (e.g., teacher, extras teachers, lunch personnel, office staff, etc.)
- Preferential seating in the front of class (so that children aren't turning around and visibly staring at them when they talk) or next to conversational partners (kids they already speak to)
- Alternative communication strategies for oral presentations/group projects, including taping the presentation and showing the teacher or allowing the child to present only to the teacher or a small group of peers
- Taping verbal homework at home
- Thoughtful peer pairing on group work
- Thoughtful class placement (considering both the teacher's interaction style and peer pairing)
- Small group testing, extended time for assessments or assessments in a private room
- The district will provide faculty training through consultations and attendance at SM conferences, as well as applicable books
- Child should not be punished and/or criticized because of the lack of speech
- Child will not be held accountable for participation points in class, or will be allowed to demonstrate class participation through other avenues of communication
- Home/school communication of brave work and speech practices on a daily or weekly basis
- School to provide quarterly parent/faculty meetings to update and report on accommodations and progress
- Child will not be called on in class without a plan or permission
- Child will be allowed to sit next to preferred peer at lunch
- Teachers will check in with the student and confirm whether the student has any questions about the assignment instead of waiting for the student to ask

Middle/High School

- All or some of the example services listed above for Elementary School
- Student will be able to meet with all teachers during their planning period during first few weeks of school
- Foreign language requirement will be waived
- Student will have alternative presentation options (alone with teacher, small group, video or audiotaped, etc.)
- Student will be allowed a private location for changing clothes during physical education class

Students who have IEPs are eligible for individualized intervention and they may work with one or more specialists at the school. Parents are encouraged to consider which interventions might be the most helpful for their child. Who would be a good fit therapeutically? Who would be a good fit in terms of personality and time? Common interventionists who can be written into the IEP include:

"Ask not what the school can do for you, but what can you do for the school!" You are asking the school to "do for you" and your child. If you can help the school that will go a long way in ultimately helping your child. In some ways, the school team may need to go out of their way to help your child overcome SM. Help them, help you!

- **Speech-language pathologist** – to increase and/or improve a child's speech and/or carry out behavioral interventions
- **Social worker** – to address a child's anxiety through behavioral interventions
- **Educational consultant** – to assist students, parents, and teachers in determining a helpful curriculum and guiding the educational experience for a child regarding academic matters
- **Behavioral analyst** – to conduct a functional behavior analysis and help develop a behavioral intervention plan based on a child's specific needs
- **Resource room teacher** – to provide a child with individualized attention for academic needs
- **School psychologist** – to address anxiety through behavioral interventions and/or consult with other service providers on effective interventions in the school setting

As noted before, private schools are not mandated by law to provide special education services. However, private schools are typically provided with a small amount of federal money each year to develop Instructional Service Plans (ISPs). It is up to the private school to determine what services they can and are willing to provide. Many private schools are willing to assign a keyworker to help children with selective mutism, as long as it is a current staff member. Therefore, parents of children in private schools may need to be more flexible with the staff who might work with their child (think outside of the box!). Parents might consider paying for educational material (books, training manuals, and training videos) for that individual. Hiring a therapist with SM expertise to work with the selected staff member, either remotely or at school, is also an option worth considering.

7 Progress Reviewed

It is important that parents receive regular feedback from the keyworker. What is the child accomplishing, how is the child progressing, and how frequently is the intervention taking place? You might consider having a three-ring binder that can be passed back and forth between parents, teachers, the keyworker, other interventionists and the outside psychologist. This way, every team member knows what others are working on, parents can appropriately reinforce and reward brave behavior at home for what occurred at school, and the team can more comprehensively evaluate the effectiveness of the intervention. Other ways of communicating can also be effective, such as a shared online document or regular emails to the team. Frequent team meetings (in person or via phone call), may also be helpful to update progress, maintain gains, and develop new short-term goals.

8 Needs Re-evaluated

IEPs, Section 504 Plans, and unofficial accommodation plans are typically updated yearly in order to determine effectiveness of the intervention and develop new short and long-term goals. These progress meetings also provide an opportunity to discuss how the child is doing and what changes need to be made at school and at home. Again, parents have the right to bring outside individuals to these meetings, including therapists or other caregivers.

> Every three years, it is required that the school fully re-evaluate children with IEPs to determine if they still meet the criteria to receive services.

Thankfully, many children with SM improve so much after effective intervention that there will come a point at which they no longer need (or qualify for) services. This is a great outcome, and it is important that parents do not fear reaching it! A formal IEP may no longer be needed when the child is able to fully engage in the classroom demands, including doing oral presentations, speaking to teachers, answering questions, talking to peers, and advocating for themselves when they are hurt, confused, ill, and/or in need of help. They may not be a social butterfly or the most outgoing child in their class, but they are progressing as expected at school. It may still be important for them to have a few specific accommodations, including a well-chosen teacher, seeing the classroom and meeting the teacher before the beginning of the school year. They may also continue to require a little extra time to answer questions and careful consideration of alternative public speaking opportunities. However, most of these can be negotiated with the school without having a formal IEP in place.

Some schools may feel "burdened" by IEPs because they are under federal mandate to provide individualized services to many students with diverse needs. For this reason, it may be in the "best interest" of the school to close out an IEP if they do not perceive a child to be significantly behind academically or socially, and parents may find themselves being encouraged to sign off. If you feel as though ending the IEP might put your child at risk of losing important and necessary services and/or accommodations, continue to advocate for your child. It will be important for parents to demonstrate how SM continues to impact their child at school, even if they've made some progress. On the other hand, many parents aren't ready to let go of the IEP "security blanket" even though their child is perfectly capable of carrying on quite well without an IEP. In both situations outlined above, a 504 Plan may be a great fit. It still provides accommodations and some special assistance for your child but it is much less formal.

* **Contact an educational advocate.** An advocate will help you understand your rights and how to advocate for services. They typically work directly with the school on your behalf. Advocates can be found via referrals or by searching "educational advocate (*your state*)." Most advocates are paid, but some provide free or low-cost services for families.

* **Request an Independent Educational Evaluation (IEE).** Parents who are uncomfortable or in disagreement with the school's findings during the evaluation may request an Independent Educational Evaluation (IEE), where the evaluation is conducted by an outside psychologist (not associated with the school) to provide a second opinion. The fee for the IEE is typically covered by the school district.

* **Request mediation.** The Individuals with Disabilities Education Act (IDEA) requires that schools provide mediation for free, upon request. A mediator is a neutral professional who works with parents and the school to find a solution. The mediator typically meets with the parents and the school at the school office and works to bring the two sides to an agreement. Because this is a formal process under IDEA law, the decision at the end of mediation is legally binding for both parties.

* **Consult with an attorney.** The attorney may have additional special education law knowledge and may be able to assist with next steps. They might suggest a due process complaint, which is a semi-formal hearing with an impartial hearing officer who decides if your child is eligible for services. Due process complaints can be complex legal procedures, so it is recommended that parents do not take this step without trying all other means first.

What is a parent's role in the school intervention?

Many parents wonder how much they should be involved in the intervention taking place at the school. There is no one size fits all answer for this; a family must take several things into consideration.

1. **How old is the child?** The older the child, the less the parent should be involved.
2. **Does the child speak to any adults in the school already?** If the child already speaks to a few people at school, the parent may need to be less involved. If the child will not speak to anyone except parents in school, they may need to assist at the start of the intervention to transfer speech to the keyworker or teacher.
3. **Is the school team engaged and consistently providing services?** Parents should be involved in the creation of the intervention plan, as well as tracking how frequently the intervention is occurring and how

"successful" the intervention appears to be. If the school is unable or unwilling to provide intervention services regularly or the child seems to be making little progress, parents may need to consider providing some of the intervention themselves (assuming the school will allow for this), such as helping to extend speech to new communication partners and to new locations at school and helping to set goals for the child.

The most important role for parents to play is that of cheerleader! As the cheerleader you are your child's most fierce advocate and their number one fan! You will also need to make sure that services are being consistently implemented in school, track data on effectiveness, and help communicate between the school and outside therapy services. If you, as a parent, have social anxiety or an introverted personality, it may be hard to engage in all of these roles. Seek out support for yourself, whether it is a friend or family member who can attend meetings with you, or a therapist of your own to increase confidence and decrease anxiety.

Providing your child with an ideal learning environment is no easy task. The handouts, worksheets, and examples that we provide should assist you with this process and save you time. They will not magically transform your child's educational experience, but they will help the school team to better understand selective mutism and what they can do to help your child!

IEP Eligibility Category Request Form

Name _____

Disability Category:

The following disability categories are the most common for children working to overcome selective mutism.

☐ **Speech/Language Impairment (SLI)**

Defined as a communication disorder which adversely affects a child's learning. A language disorder "may be characterized by difficulty in understanding and producing language, including word meanings (semantics), the components of words (morphology), the components of sentences (syntax), or the conventions of conversation (pragmatics)" (Head Start, 2006). Children with Selective Mutism may have primary disabilities in speech (including semantics, articulation, and fluency), but also have social pragmatic speech weaknesses (the ability to utilize speech effectively in social situations).

☐ **Other Health Impairment (OHI)**

Defined as a child who has a chronic or acute health condition which limits alertness in the educational environment due to either limited strength, vitality, and alertness or heightened alertness to the surrounding environment; these must impair academic performance (Grice, 2002).

☐ **Emotional Disturbance/Disability (ED)**

Defined as a child whose education is impacted by one or more of the following emotional or behavioral issues:

A. An inability to learn that cannot be explained by intellectual, sensory, or health factors.
B. An inability to build or maintain satisfactory interpersonal relationships with peers and teachers.
C. Inappropriate types of behavior or feelings under normal circumstances.
D. A general pervasive mood of unhappiness or depression.
E. A tendency to develop physical symptoms or fears associated with personal or school problems.

Notes:

Caregiver Note: The category for eligibility will typically be chosen by the team deciding eligibility. If you disagree with the category selected, you may request that another category be chosen. Most children with SM will fit nicely into the Speech/Language Impairment category or the Other Health Impaired category.

Consideration of Special Education Services
IEP Request Letter

Everything between the brackets should be customized. Be sure to edit content in order to reflect your child's specific situation. Send a copy to the principal/special education director of the program and keep a copy for yourself.

[Date]
[Special Education Director Name or Principal's Name]
[Address]
[City, State, Zip Code]

Dear [Special Education Director's Name or Principal's Name]:

My child, [child's name], is currently in [list program or grade] at [school name]. Given a recent diagnosis of selective mutism, a specific anxiety disorder, I would like my child to be evaluated for special education services. I would also appreciate the chance to meet with the special education team to discuss [his/her] current placement situation and to look at how we can modify [his/her] current goals and objectives to better fit [his/her] educational needs.

[Edit this paragraph to reflect your specific situation] Despite attempts to increase speech in the school setting, my child continues to struggle with significant anxiety which impacts [his/her] ability to focus, learn, and fully participate in the academic setting. [He/She] cannot participate verbally in the classroom, and therefore is not able to do oral presentations, group projects, paired activities, etc. Additionally, [he/she] cannot alert the teacher if [he/she] doesn't understand, needs help, or is hurt/sick.

Research demonstrates that children with selective mutism are very successful when they have specific intervention and accommodation plans in the school setting. This includes identifying and working with a specific individual "keyworker" who can help the child practice "being brave" and encourage speech with multiple individuals in new environments.

Please schedule a meeting as soon as possible so that we can discuss these issues and consider appropriate interventions and accommodations. I would prefer being contacted with time options in advance so that a team meeting can be scheduled at a mutually agreeable time and place. I understand that the school has 45 school days to evaluate my child and hold the eligibility meeting.

I look forward to hearing from you soon and working together to help [child's name].

Sincerely,

[Parent/Guardian Name]
[Address]
[City, State, Zip Code]
[Phone Number]

IEP Meeting Notes

Name_____ Grade/Age_____ Date_____

SCHOOL TEAM INFORMATION:

Attendees:

Assigned Keyworker:

Next Meeting Date:

NOTES:

FOLLOW-UP:

My to-do list:

School team to-do list:

IEP Goal Planning *Example*

Name ___*Bailey Brown*___ Grade/Age___*2nd/7*___ Date___*9/15/18*___

Annual Goal #: *3*

Goals should be specific, easily measureable, realistic, relevant, assessable, and given a specific end date.

Student will speak in a full voice with the general education teacher in the general education classroom by June of 2019.

Short Term Objectives:

Short term objectives help track progress toward the annual goal. They may be viewed as checkpoints.

1. *By November, when asked a forced-choice question by the teacher in private, student will respond verbally with 90% consistency*
2. *By January, when asked a forced-choice question by the teacher in a small-group activity, student will respond with 90% consistency*
3. *By March, when asked an open-ended question by the teacher in a small-group setting, student will answer with 90% consistency*
4. *By May, when asked either a forced-choice or open-ended question by the teacher in the classroom setting, student will respond with 90% consistency*

Classroom Accommodations:

What accommodations will be necessary to achieve this goal?

* ☀ *Preferential Seating*
* ☀ *One-on-one brave work practice with teacher*
* ☀ *Advanced notice and role playing for speech prompts*
* ☀ *Carefully-chosen peer groups for group work*

SPECIAL SERVICES (OT, SLP, ETC.):

Will special services be required to achieve this goal? Check all that apply.

- ☑ Speech language pathologist (to increase and/or improve my child's speech and/or carry out behavioral interventions)
- ☑ Social worker (to address my child's anxiety through behavioral interventions)
- ❑ Educational consultant (to assist in creating a helpful curriculum or educational experience for my child)
- ❑ Behavioral analyst (to conduct a functional behavior analysis and help develop a behavioral intervention plan based on my child's specific needs)
- ❑ Resource room teacher (to provide my child with individualized attention for academic needs)
- ❑ School Psychologist (to address anxiety through behavioral interventions and/or consult with other service providers on effective interventions in the school setting)

- ❑ Other:_____

Notes:

* ☀ *It will be important for the teacher to develop a positive rapport with the student first*
* ☀ *Student really enjoys questions about dinosaurs – teacher should focus forced-choice questions on this area of interest first*
* ☀ *Teacher will be giving stickers discretely to child for each successful brave practice, to be cashed in at home for prizes*
* ☀ *If student does not answer, teacher will wait 5 seconds and then ask again*
* ☀ *School personnel will read books and websites on how to effectively interact with children with Selective Mutism*

IEP Goal Planning

Annual Goal #:

Goals should be specific, easily measureable, realistic, relevant, assessable, and given a specific end date.

Short Term Objectives:

Short term objectives help track progress toward the annual goal. They may be viewed as checkpoints.

Classroom Accommodations:

What accommodations will be necessary to achieve this goal?

SPECIAL SERVICES (OT, SLP, ETC.):

Will special services be required to achieve this goal? Check all that apply.

- ❑ Speech language pathologist (to increase and/or improve my child's speech and/or carry out behavioral interventions)
- ❑ Social worker (to address my child's anxiety through behavioral interventions)
- ❑ Educational consultant (to assist in creating a helpful curriculum or educational experience for my child)
- ❑ Behavioral analyst (to conduct a functional behavior analysis and help develop a behavioral intervention plan based on my child's specific needs)
- ❑ Resource room teacher (to provide my child with individualized attention for academic needs)
- ❑ School Psychologist (to address anxiety through behavioral interventions and/or consult with other service providers on effective interventions in the school setting)

- ❑ Other:_____

Notes:

Services/Accomodations Goal Tracking *Example*

Name _____ *Bailey Brown* _____ Grade/Age ____ *2nd/7* ____

Service/Accommodation:

Speech & Language, Mrs. White

Goal:

Student will speak in a full voice with the general education teacher in the general education classroom by June of 2019.

Date	Activity	Duration	Notes
9/25/18	Played games in resource room	30 min.	See Brave Work Log
10/1/18	Established speech with me	30 min.	See Brave Work Log
10/8/18	Played games with Ms. Ro and me in resource room	30 min.	See Brave Work Log
10/10/18	Team meeting with Ms. Ro, Mr. Paul, and Mrs. Rodgers	30 min.	Discussed what is working and provided recommendations, see note in folder
10/17/18	Classroom teacher, Bailey, and me in resource room. Fade in activity.	30 min.	Successful fade in! Bailey whispered. More info on Brave Work Log

Services/Accomodations Goal Tracking

Name _____ Grade/Age_____

Service/Accommodation:

Goal:

Date	Activity	Duration	Notes

Getting to Know Me! *Example*

Name ___Diego Garcia___   Grade/Age ___2nd/8___   Date ___8/15/19___

What is selective mutism (SM)?

Selective mutism is a childhood anxiety disorder characterized by a child's inability to speak and communicate effectively in *select* social situations, such as school. Children with SM are able to speak and communicate in settings where they are comfortable, secure, and relaxed (usually with their family at home).

Is selective mutism a matter of discipline?

Although the word "selective" may seem as though a child has a choice in the matter, SM is not as simple as a child being shy or refusing to talk and it is not something for which a child can be "disciplined". They may seem withdrawn or uncomfortable. This is NOT because they are unhappy, purposely ignoring you or trying to get attention. It is because the child is so consumed by anxiety and fear that they cannot speak. They can and WILL speak when the right techniques are employed.

Why do children develop SM?

SM is currently understood as a type of social anxiety and children with SM may have a fear of others hearing their voice. It is believed to have genetic, biological, environmental and temperamental components. It is **NOT** caused by trauma, abuse, or bad parenting.

SM impacts each child very differently, however some common impacts include:

* Difficulty speaking in the school environment
* Inability to make eye contact, awkward/stiff body language, non-verbal communication, etc.
* Situational avoidance in speaking with neighbors, unfamiliar adults and children, and even some relatives outside of the immediate family
* Struggling to speak in environments and with people where there is a history of avoidance
* Difficulty in starting new activities and meeting new people

About Me:

My name is Diego and I enjoy all things SHARK! I love Star Wars and playing with my little brother too. I recently started building a big Lego set and I can't wait to finish it. I'm really quiet at school but I'm not at all shy. I have two friends on my street that I speak with at home and we can get quite rambunctious together!

I am Overcoming Selective Mutism:

I DO speak (and a lot) when I feel comfortable with my surroundings. I enjoy the company of my peers and I am able to speak comfortably with most children. However, I still have great difficulty speaking with adults. It is essential that you provide me with ample and appropriate opportunities to use my voice particularly during our first interactions so that I don't get too comfortable staying silent.

Important Notes:

* *I understand that all people have challenges that they work to overcome and that every child is "working" on something. I know that my challenge is using my voice in some situations.*

* *While I am aware that I have to work hard to speak, I am unaware and unfamiliar with the term selective mutism. Please do not question me as to why I don't speak and don't punish me for not speaking.*

* *When I do speak to you, roll with it and do NOT draw attention, act surprised, or praise me. This could embarrass me and cause a set back.*

* *I may not ask when I need help.*

PRIVATE: DO NOT SHARE WITHOUT PERMISSION

Learn more about selective mutism: selectivemutism.org childmind.org selectivemutismlearning.org

Getting to Know Me!

What is selective mutism (SM)?

Selective mutism is a childhood anxiety disorder characterized by a child's inability to speak and communicate effectively in *select* social situations, such as school. Children with SM are able to speak and communicate in settings where they are comfortable, secure, and relaxed (usually with their family at home).

Is selective mutism a matter of discipline?

Although the word "selective" may seem as though a child has a choice in the matter, SM is not as simple as a child being shy or refusing to talk and it is not something for which a child can be "disciplined". They may seem withdrawn or uncomfortable. This is NOT because they are unhappy, purposely ignoring you or trying to get attention. It is because the child is so consumed by anxiety and fear that they cannot speak. They can and WILL speak when the right techniques are employed.

Why do children develop SM?

SM is currently understood as a type of social anxiety and children with SM may have a fear of others hearing their voice. It is believed to have genetic, biological, environmental and temperamental components. It is **NOT** caused by trauma, abuse, or bad parenting.

SM impacts each child very differently, however some common impacts include:

* Difficulty speaking in the school environment
* Inability to make eye contact, awkward/stiff body language, non-verbal communication, etc.
* Situational avoidance in speaking with neighbors, unfamiliar adults and children, and even some relatives outside of the immediate family
* Struggling to speak in environments and with people where there is a history of avoidance
* Difficulty in starting new activities and meeting new people

About Me:

I am Overcoming Selective Mutism:

Important Notes:

PRIVATE: DO NOT SHARE WITHOUT PERMISSION

Learn more about selective mutism: selectivemutism.org ❋ childmind.org ❋ selectivemutismlearning.org

Quick Tips for Successful Communication

Decreasing anxiety and creating a relaxed setting for a child to speak

| To BEGIN (Warm-up): | EXAMPLES: | POINTERS: |

1

Make one sided conversation like a "sportscaster" and AVOID asking questions. *Speak by making statements that do not require "answers".*

❂ *I love how you are coloring your princess pink. Oh, look at that, you added a nice castle for your princess.*

❂ *I brought my lunch today and I can't wait to eat my bologna sandwich and pretzels!*

❂ Avoid Yes/No questions because they can lead to head nodding and the child should be encouraged to use their voice.

AFTER the Warm-up: EXAMPLES:

2

Speak normally, asking "forced-choice" questions that require a brief answer, and pause for a response, if necessary. *Allow for hesitation (at least 5 seconds).*

❂ *Would you like to use blue, purple or another color for your project?*

❂ *Did you bring your lunch or are you buying lunch today?*

❂ Teachers should gradually structure interactions in a way that fosters verbalization rather than nonverbal communication.

3

If there is no response, please repeat the question. *Don't act disappointed or anxious if there is no response. Allow for hesitation (at least 5 seconds).*

❂ *Would you like to use blue, purple or another color for your project?*

❂ *Did you bring your lunch or are you buying lunch today?*

"I see you shaking your head but I'd like you to use your voice."

❂ Do not forget to allow at least 5 seconds for the child to respond.

4

If there is still no answer, reframe the question into a yes or no question so that it can be answered non-verbally. *Move back into sports casting and try a forced choice question again later.*

❂ *Would you like purple? Yes or No?*

❂ *Did you bring your lunch today? Yes or No?*

❂ If these steps don't work, check in with the child's parents/therapist for next steps.

ESSENTIAL Reminders:

❂ Please do **NOT** avoid interacting with children who have SM, but do avoid asking questions at first.

❂ Do **NOT** ask them why they don't speak or try to make them speak. Both of these tactics can increase anxiety and can ultimately delay speech.

❂ If others ask why they don't speak (**OR** why they whisper), please correct them and let them know that they do speak (speak louder) when they are ready. Especially important if they ask in front of the child!

❂ Teachers should redirect when peers speak for the child (this may accidentally rescue the child from communicating). Teachers may consider pulling the child with SM aside to ask privately what they need in order to get direct speech or communication. If the child is unable to speak to you directly, check with parents/therapist to determine if it is acceptable for the child to use a peer as a "verbal intermediary".

❂ When they **DO** speak, please **DO NOT** act surprised or draw attention to the occurrence. Acting surprised or overly excited when they do speak might cause the child to withdraw.

Chapter Seven

CONQUERING CHALLENGES: PRACTICE, REINFORCE, REPEAT

Central to overcoming selective mutism is developing an overall plan that will slowly help your child reach increasingly difficult goals. When thinking about which pathways to focus on, consider the situations in which your child struggles. Do they struggle in specific environments, with certain people or when certain expectations are placed on their speech? In this chapter, we present a series of handouts and examples to help you better focus your efforts to create a tailored plan for your child. We offer examples of how to complete each handout, but we encourage you to use the blank copies at the end of the chapter as you carefully consider your child's individual goals. The older and more mature your child is, the more you may wish to involve them in the planning process (being careful not to overwhelm them). It's time to reach for the top of Peers Peak, School Summit, Community Crest, and Mount Mindful! Practice, reinforce, repeat… As you start planning challenge pathways for/with your child, consider that each pathway will provide a step-wise approach to meeting a specific milestone. Begin to think about situations you would like to help your child conquer, and which steps they will need to accomplish in order to reach the end of a particular pathway. We list several common challenges in our example of the *Goal Mapping* worksheet but these are just a handful of the many challenges that children with SM might be working to overcome. Are these challenges relevant for your child?

It is also important to explore Pathway Hazards, or factors that may influence your child's progress while planning. In chapter 3 we introduced the Pathway Hazards – (1) the audience, (2) the environment and (3) the speech demand. In chapter 4 we asked you to consider which factors influence your child's ability to speak and communicate. When considering which challenge your child may be ready to take on, think about these factors as they might be helpful in determining the appropriate order of steps to reach important goals.

Reflect back on the *Cataloguing Current Speaking Abilities and Challenges* worksheet from chapter 4 (if you had a chance to complete it) and ask yourself the following questions:

Goal Mapping
Worksheet
This may be helpful for
considering which goals
your child may need to
work toward.

Challenge
Pathway Planning
Encourages parents to
plan slow, consistent steps
toward a speaking goal.

* How can my child grow in the number of *people* with whom they speak? Who might we add on as a communication partner? Are they novel or known to the child? Will they practice private responses, small group responding, or speaking with a larger/public audience?

* How can my child increase the number of *places* where they speak? Are there any environments that are particularly difficult for your child? Do environmental stimuli impact their speech (e.g. crowded and noisy vs quiet)?

* How can my child increase in their verbalization? Do they need to use a louder voice? Should they be working on longer answers? Do they seem to have more trouble initiating or responding to speech?

Now that you have identified several goals/challenges for your child, begin to think about which goals might be the most attainable. The *Challenge Pathway Planning* worksheet provides space for planning appropriate steps to reach an intended goal. Notice that we include space for you to consider Pathway Hazards on this worksheet so that it will be easier for you to think through possible steps to help your child meet their goal. Perhaps it's easier for your child to speak in a quiet and less chaotic environment rather than a crowded environment or maybe it's easier to speak with girls and women than with boys or men. Use that knowledge and carefully consider these factors when planning pathways so that you are creating opportunities for success.

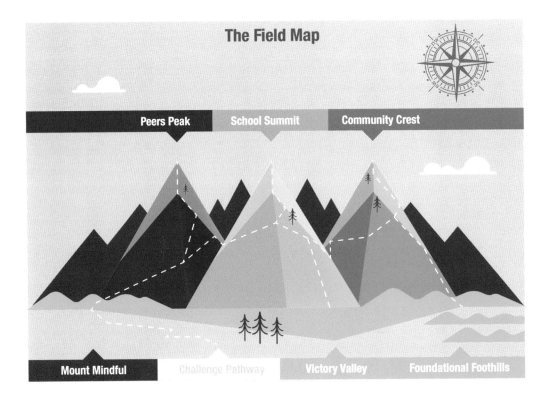

Goal Mapping *Example*

Determining Goals - Which situations are challenging for your child?

Use the open space below to list challenging situations that your child faces with peers, at school, and in the community.   Which Mount Mindful skills might be important to explore?

- *Participating in small group conversations*
- *Talking on the phone to friends*
- *Speaking with peers at extracurricular activities*
- *Speaking at playdates at home*
- *Responding to peers at a public playground*

- *Speaking to a friend one on one*
- *Answering the teacher*
- *Asking the teacher for help*
- *Presenting in front of the class*
- *Speaking with specials teachers*
- *Speaking in small groups*

- *Asking for a free sample at the grocery*
- *Ordering at a restaurant*
- *Responding to healthcare workers*
- *Speaking to coaches*
- *Responding when approached unexpectedly*
- *Speaking with extended family members*

- *The more you do, the more you can do (small steps = big accomplishments)*
- *Comfort with being uncomfortable*
- *Perfection is a problem*
- *Staying with challenges - grit*

*This is not an exhaustive list of challenges faced by children with SM. These are examples to help you formulate a plan for your child

Notes:

Challenge Pathway *Example*

Responding to peers at a public playground...

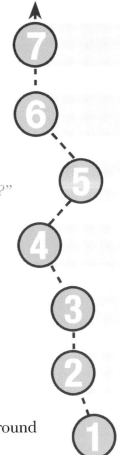

Child is prompted to ask the peer a scripted question
Example: *"Why don't you ask our friend, how old are you?."*

Parent continues to prompt the peer to ask questions
Example: *"Can you ask my daughter how old she is?."*

Parent prompts the peer to ask the child a forced-choice question
Example: *"My daughter has a favorite slide too, can you ask her if she likes the big or the small slide?"*

Parent engages the peer
Example: *"Do you like the big slide or the small slide?"*

Adult prompts for speech within earshot of the peer
Example: *"Do you want to go on the big slide or the small slide?"*

Adult speaks to another child (a peer) in order to bring them into the interaction
Example: *Parent notices a peer playing by the slide and moves with child near the slide*

Adult encourages the child to be comfortable and verbal (with them) at the playground
Example: *Parent plays with child on the swings and might ask the child how fast they want to swing*

Which Factors might influence progress?

THE AUDIENCE

- *This interaction should be private with no other adults present (could make it harder)*

- *It's best if the peer is a girl*

THE ENVIRONMENT

- *We should go to Liberty Park because it tends to be quiet*

- *It's best if it's not too cold when we do the challenge*

THE SPEECH DEMAND

- *Start with forced-choice questions and then move on to basic questions with one word answers.*

- *If she whispers, that's ok. We can work on volume later.*

Notes

- *I need to remember that every child progresses at a different pace. She may be able to move through all of these steps in one interaction, or she may be practicing a specific step over a longer period of time. Steps may need to be adjusted or re-ordered. I won't know until we try!*

- *If peers ask why she doesn't talk, or if she freezes, I should say, "She speaks when she is comfortable, and she is practicing speaking to new friends. Sometimes learning new things takes time!"*

There are many strategies for advancing a child's comfort with speaking confidently in new places and with new people. Fundamental to each strategy is not only practicing frequently but seeking out activities and demands that are slightly higher than your child's current comfort level, while being careful not to change too many factors at once. Establishing appropriate steps, goals and expectations for your child's brave work is perhaps the most important aspect in making it easier for your child to overcome a challenge.

Peers Peak
Conquering Playdates

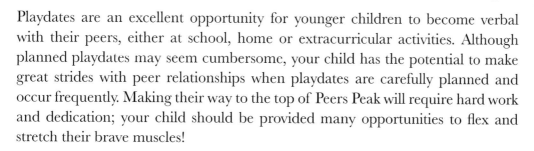

Playdates are an excellent opportunity for younger children to become verbal with their peers, either at school, home or extracurricular activities. Although planned playdates may seem cumbersome, your child has the potential to make great strides with peer relationships when playdates are carefully planned and occur frequently. Making their way to the top of Peers Peak will require hard work and dedication; your child should be provided many opportunities to flex and stretch their brave muscles!

Dynamics of a Successful Playdate

Planning and Leadership - *A playdate with a new child will require parent/teacher/therapist involvement to plan and lead the interaction so that the child will have fun, feel successful, and look forward to future get-togethers. The adult should take great care to select appropriate interactive activities that will encourage speaking (arts and crafts, games, cooking, pretend play, kitchen activities, etc.).*

Carefully Selected Peers - *Many times children with SM will seek out playmates who are quick to respond, but that may not be the best choice for a "learning" playdate. Patience is a necessity during these planned encounters. A good choice will be a child who is slightly more mature than their peers, conversationally self-reliant but not "pushy" and who will have the patience to wait for a response from your child.*

Relaxed Environment - *Choose a familiar, comfortable environment where the child is mostly verbal. That might be at home, the playground, or somewhere else. A new environment may inhibit communication especially if it is a location where the child is accustomed to not speaking. For example, if the child is not verbal in the classroom, do not choose the classroom for a playdate. Perhaps the library or a resource room is more comfortable for your child and would increase the likelihood of success.*

Appropriate Expectations - *When planning the playdate, take time to consider the challenge pathway progression. Think through the steps your child might take in order to meet the goal of a particular playdate or challenge. The goal might be to simply play with a peer (nonverbally), respond to a peer at a one-on-one playdate, initiate with a peer during a playdate or participate in a conversation with a group of peers, etc. There are many pathways that children may take while working to conquer "Peers Peak". In most cases, children will have many playdates and conquer many different challenges before it becomes easier and more natural for them to communicate conversationally with peers.*

These are new skills for both parents and children and therefore mistakes may happen, and you might not get it exactly right the first time or every time, but both you and your child will become more skilled with practice.

Impactful Peer Interactions Worksheet
This worksheet will assist parents in planning and organizing successful playdates with peers.

Impactful Peer Interactions *Example*
Conquering Playdates

Peers

Select peers who are patient, well-liked and helpful (ask the teacher to provide a list if necessary). We recommend beginning with one-on-one interactions. Once the child has conquered one-on-one interactions, small group activities might be next.

Jill – Everyone loves Jill, she just loves to be helpful and she seems older than she is.

Rebecca – She a social butterfly, she's really smart and she follows directions.

Which peer(s) will take part in this interaction and what should they understand prior to the interaction?

Rebecca is a good choice for this interaction. I will tell her that we are going to play games with Sam during lunch. I will let her know that Sam likes to talk but she has to feel comfortable first so she might be quiet for a while. I will also warn her not to make a big deal about Sam talking or ask why she doesn't because it might embarrass her. I'll ask Rebecca to just keep playing and talking to her anyway.

Plan

Where will the interaction be?

In the room next to the classroom during lunch. It will be best if there aren't any distractions

What will the children be doing?

They will play "Let's Go Fishing" for warm up because it doesn't require speaking and the kids can have fun with it. Then we'll play "Pop-Up Pirate".

What will you do to help facilitate?

When the kids play "Let's Go Fishing" I'll be the sportscaster and say things like, "Oh, great job grabbing the orange fish, Sam!" and "Wow, that was quick Rebecca!". When we switch to "Pop-Up Pirate", let both kids know that when they put their sword into the barrel, they should say the color of the sword. I'll be prepared to wait five seconds for Sam to say the color, but if she doesn't, I'll ask, "Is that the red sword or the blue sword?"

Outcome & Notes

What worked well? Does anything need to be adjusted for the next interaction? Any breakthroughs?

Let's Go Fishing was fun! Sam was apprehensive but whispered "Blue" in front of Rebecca! I didn't prompt her to say it louder but next time, I will do that. I think I'd like to do this type of activity a few more times (this week and next) with some of her other peers and see if we can get Sam to increase her volume and then perhaps use more than one word when she responds.

Breakthrough – whispering with a peer present!!

School Summit
Making communication gains at school

The school setting can present a myriad of challenges for children with SM. School can be a perfect storm of anxiety– social stress, the desire to be perfect, unpredictable schedules, and many novel adults. While it's important to address anxiety in the school setting, it can be difficult to do so for a variety of reasons (addressed in chapter 6). Even though school is typically the location where children struggle the most, parents and teachers can set up strategic challenges to help children face their fears in slow, steady steps. In this section, we include an example challenge pathway highlighting the steps to reach a higher-level goal in the school setting (*Presenting in front of the class*). We encourage you to use the resources provided in chapter 6 as you plan for speech success at school.

Presenting in Front of the Class
Challenge Pathway Example

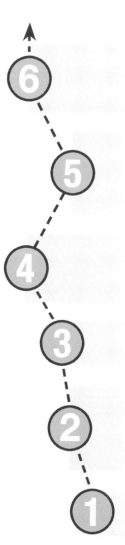

Child completes the presentation in same manner as her peers.
Example: Child performs her presentation in front of the class, in random order, with minimal reference to notecards and with questions at the end.

With careful planning, the child performs the same presentation in front of her class. Example: *The child will do her presentation in front of the class but the order will be carefully determined ahead of time and she will be allowed to read from notecards if she wishes. No follow up questions will be asked.*

Child performs the same presentation in front of the teacher and a few chosen peers. Example: *During lunch, the child, the teacher, and 3 friends meet and the child does the presentation.*

Child performs the same presentation in front of the teacher privately.
Example: Child stays after school and does the presentation for the teacher

Child watches the presentation video with the teacher, and the teacher comments on the presentation. Example: *Child and teacher watch the presentation together and the teacher comments, "I like how you described the difference between slate and volcanic rock."*

Child videotapes the presentation and allows the teacher to watch it privately.
Example: Parent videotapes the child's science project presentation.

Think about the goal you are trying to help your child meet and determine a few ways each week to work toward that goal. Use the challenge pathway worksheets to help track progress toward the current goal. You may also choose to use the brave work log to keep track of daily practices; this can be passed back and forth between the school, home, and the therapist.

Brave Work Log

This document is best used when intervention activities and challenge pathways are being completed with several adults. The log will allow interventionists to pass along valuable notes about progress via a shared document (like a google drive document), a folder, or a 3-ring binder. Use this document to share information on the frequency, difficulty level, and outcomes of brave work.

To set goals and objectives for community brave work, it is important that once again we keep in mind the three factors that determine difficulty level: 1) the audience, 2) the environment, and 3) the speech demand. *Planned, scripted speech* in public situations is much easier than *unexpected, spontaneous* interactions. Parents are encouraged to consider which public activities or errands could be adapted to serve as possible brave work opportunities. For example, does your family need to go to the post office to get stamps? Depending on your child's level of speech, perhaps they could:

- Wave and/or smile at the employee (nonverbal gesture)
- Hand over money or credit card (nonverbal interaction)
- Answer how many stamps you need (one-word, concrete, scripted response)
- Answer what you need and how many (multiple word scripted response, such as "I need 6 stamps")
- Add in polite words, including please and thank you
- Verbally handle the entire interaction with the employee, with the parents scripting prior to the interaction what the child will need to ask, such as '"Do you have any flower stamps" as well as help the child anticipate follow-up questions (scripted initiation)
- Approach and handle the entire interaction independently, with no prompting or scripting from the parent (spontaneous initiation)

There are many opportunities for practicing in public, depending on the skill level, age, and interests of your child. Brave practices might include:

- Store scavenger hunt – finding items on a list by asking employees for their location in the store
- Ordering at restaurants
- Talking to peers on the playground
- Talking at the post office
- Asking questions at the pet store or craft store
- Asking for help finding a book at the library
- Selling something door to door
- Responding to employees at do-it-yourself pottery or painting stores

Ordering at a Restaurant
Challenge Pathway Example

Child gets the attention of the waitress to make a request
Example: *"Excuse me, can I have a refill on my water please?"*

Child begins to use etiquette and polite words
Example: *Looking at the the waiter, the child says, " I would like a hamburger and fries, please."*

Child responds to follow-up questions about their order
Example: *When the waitress asks about toppings the child responds, "Mustard and Tomato."*

Child orders using a full sentence
Example: *"I would like a hamburger and fries."*

Child orders using multiple words
Example: *"Hamburger and fries."*

Child orders using one word
Example: *"Hamburger."*

Adult helps the child identify what they want to order and identifies the goal for ordering
Example: *"You want a hamburger, fries, and a sprite. You say hamburger and I'll say the rest."*

Parent engages the child in playful, relaxed speech at the restaurant table
Example: *Wasn't the movie today amazing? What did you like the best?"*

Community Crest
Unexpected or unplanned practice in public

Unexpected or unplanned brave practices in public can make for great opportunities, but parents should know how to prompt appropriately and reduce expectations if necessary (picking battles or reducing the goal). In a perfect world, you would be able to precisely control the situations, the prompts, and the people involved. In that perfect world, all interactions would take into account your child's challenge with speaking in certain situations. Expectations would be adjusted, and your child would never be asked to work past their current ability level unless they were ready. Unfortunately, that is not our reality, and you will <u>not</u> be able to control public interactions as much as you might like. Adults will approach your child <u>without</u> warning and ask them questions, make comments, and expect them to answer. Other children will enter their personal space and pepper them with

*We provide several fun, engaging worksheets for community practice, including **Pop-up People Challenge**, **Success with Important Adults**, **Person Bingo** with game cards, and the **Survey Says… Game** with example survey questions.*

questions. These situations are all out of your control! However, you do have control over two things – your expectations of the child's brave work abilities and your prompts for speech or engagement in those situations.

Because of the unplanned and unexpected nature of these interactions, we refer to the people who begin these interactions as *"pop-up people."* Since *"pop-up people"* do not know what step your child is working on, parents may need to make the brave work easier by changing the question or prompt, or even by taking the prompt away altogether. For example, if a clerk in the checkout line at a store asks your child how old she is, and your child has been practicing answering a one-word question, then this is an appropriate (albeit unplanned) brave work opportunity.

A flowchart of prompts and expected responses for this example might include:

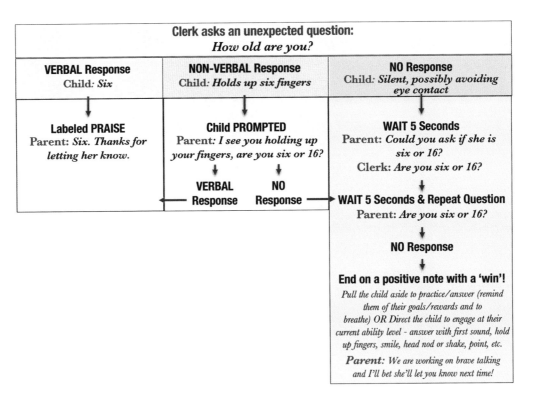

The same clerk may unexpectedly try to engage your child in a longer discussion. If their goal currently includes only one-word responses, a parent may need to step in and cut the conversation short or rephrase the clerk's questions (e.g., if the clerk asked a question that clearly would necessitate a response longer than one-word, like "Tell me about your summer vacation," the parent may need to rephrase the question to a forced-choice question requiring only a short answer, like "Did we go to the beach or Disney?"). By changing one factor, the speech demand, you are signaling to your child that you are "on their team." You are assisting them in overcoming their challenges in a way that is manageable. You have helped them in taking another step forward where they easily could have felt defeated - you changed the outcome, your child has a small victory, and you've gained their trust!

Some children are so afraid of *pop-up people* that they will avoid social or public situations where these interactions might occur, especially if they don't have anyone to "rescue" them or answer for them. Helpful strategies to engage your child in these practices (and thereby reduce their anxiety) might include:

- ☀ Setting a goal with a generous reward for engaging with *pop-up people*
- ☀ Helping your child script and practice common questions that could be asked unexpectedly. These might include how to respond to a compliment and how to respond to typical questions like, "What is your name?", "How old are you?", or "How are you doing?"
- ☀ Being ready to make the prompts or questions simpler for your child to answer (e.g., rephrase to a forced-choice question, ask a shorter or simpler question, etc.).

Preparing your child for unexpected speaking encounters will go a long way toward helping them find success in these situations. Ask them questions like, "What might the store clerks ask when we are buying groceries?" and "Who else might sometimes surprise us with questions?" and then practice these scenarios frequently.

Pop-up People Challenge and Preparing for Pop-up People practice Worksheets
These will be helpful in preparing for and directly addressing the challenge of speaking to unexpected adults (pop-up people) in public.

Preparing for Pop-up People *Example*

Instructions: We recommend that this sheet be completed and practiced (as often as possible) before the "Pop-up People Challenge" worksheet. When children are prepared for speaking, interactions will feel easier. This may be a higher level challenge for some children.

Before the challenge

What situations are challenging?	Let's practice what we will say!
When someone asks where I go to school.	Them: *Where do you go to school?* Me (basic): *Westside Elementary.* Me (advanced): *I go to Westside Elementary.*
When someone wants to know my name.	Them: *What's your name?* Me (basic): *Simon.* Me (advanced): *My name is Simon.*
When someone asks how old I am.	Them: *How old are you sweetie?* Me (basic): *7* Me (advanced): *I'm 7 years old.*
When someone asks if I like something.	Them: *Do you like chocolate chip cookies?* Me (basic): *Yes.* Me (advanced): *Yes. They are good.*
When someone asks about my red hair.	Them: *Where did you get that pretty red hair?* Me (basic): *My dad.* Me (advanced): *From my dad.*

After the challenge
We did it! What was the hardest part?

The hardest part was when people asked me things and I wasn't ready to answer yet.

We did it! What did we learn?

I learned that if I practice, it gets easier.

Pop-up People Challenge *Example*

Instructions: Use this page to track successful interactions with "pop-up people" - unexpected verbal interactions that occur in the community setting. After reaching ten successful verbal interactions, caregivers may choose to provide a special prize!

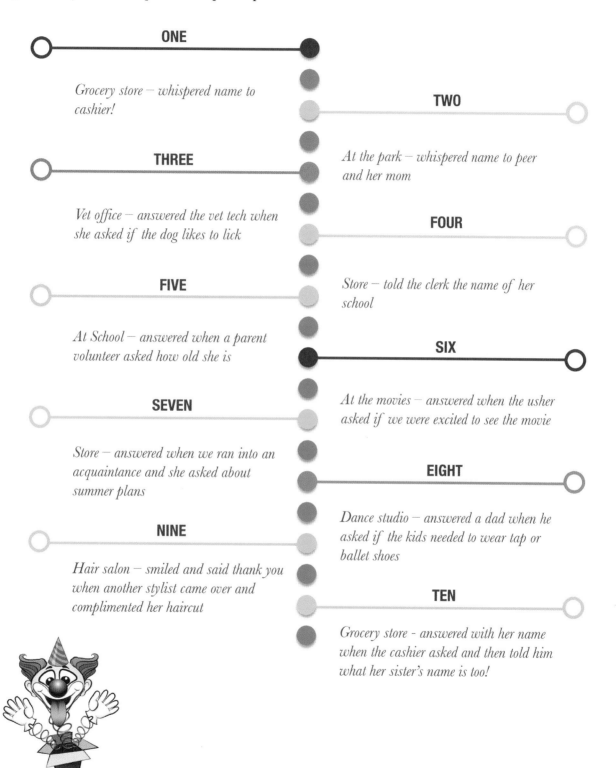

ONE

Grocery store – whispered name to cashier!

TWO

At the park – whispered name to peer and her mom

THREE

Vet office – answered the vet tech when she asked if the dog likes to lick

FOUR

Store – told the clerk the name of her school

FIVE

At School – answered when a parent volunteer asked how old she is

SIX

At the movies – answered when the usher asked if we were excited to see the movie

SEVEN

Store – answered when we ran into an acquaintance and she asked about summer plans

EIGHT

Dance studio – answered a dad when he asked if the kids needed to wear tap or ballet shoes

NINE

Hair salon – smiled and said thank you when another stylist came over and complimented her haircut

TEN

Grocery store - answered with her name when the cashier asked and then told him what her sister's name is too!

Some possible factors that might make some people more difficult to speak with than others are gender, how often the child sees/speaks to the person, how well this person's personality matches with your child, and/or the motivation of your child to speak to this person.

Many children struggle to speak with familiar adults and extended family. Creating a goal list of adults can be helpful to track *who* we want to have as a communication partner and *how* we plan to do it. This list may include coaches, family friends, extended family, religious education teachers, etc. If possible, parents should consider the difficulty level when creating the list. If your child is old enough to understand and willing to take part, include them in creating the steps in the path to speaking with the important people in their lives. They may have valuable insight into how hard it might be to speak with certain adults, who they might prefer to work with first, and who they might prefer to save for later.

Children may be more challenged by contaminated adults or peers. When a child does not talk to a specific person or in a specific place for a long period, it is increasingly more difficult for the child to speak in that situation or to that person (thus, this person or environment becomes "contaminated"). As an adult, an example that is easy to relate to is moving to a new home, where you intend to greet your new neighbors but become very busy. As weeks and months pass, you become increasingly hesitant to ring their doorbell and introduce yourself, because it is uncomfortable! "Hi, I'm your new neighbor… I moved in two years ago!" Eventually, you resign yourself to never speaking to your neighbor! Your neighbor has become contaminated.

Contamination is not the "kiss of death." It simply means that these people or environments will be more difficult because there is a long history of silence. For example, a child who did not talk to her Kindergarten teacher for an entire year may require a longer stimulus fading or shaping process to elicit speech with her new teacher. If contamination is a factor, you may wish to wait to tackle those environments, people, or situations, because they will be more easily accomplished once the child has built up their confidence by working toward other brave goals.

If your child states that they will never be able to talk to someone, don't be discouraged. Place them last in the order and reflect, "That person will be a challenge to talk with, and it feels impossible right now, but it may feel easier later. Let's put them at the end of our practice schedule."

Success with Important Adults *Example*

Who are the most challenging people to speak with?

Instructions: Discuss the people with whom your child has difficulty speaking and determine a plan for beginning to speak with these "contaminated" people. Be sure to track and reward successful interactions!

Who	Plan for Speaking	I did it!
Jack Jackson	Playdate at my house with games	DID IT!
Sheila Grover	Play "HORSE" with the basketball at church gymnasium	Basketball made it fun and easier!
Reverend Leonard	Play "HORSE" with the basketball at church gymnasium	Basketball made it fun and easier!
Ms. Laurie	Play question Jenga at the school library	It was crowded but I did it!
Mr. Luther	Play question Jenga at the school library	Easier today - it wasn't crowded
Coach Virginia	Play soccer with Coach Virginia alone and answer questions with each kick (go early before practice)	Kicking the ball was fun and helped me to talk
Mrs. Harrell	At playdate with Reed, play on IPADs and she can ask questions about the games we play	It was really hard even with my IPAD
Mary Champer	When she comes to deliver the order, ask her a question	Really nervous - asked the question anyway!
Leroy Manin	When we drop our dry cleaning, ask how much it is	It felt easy today!
Holly Bleu	Go to the art studio early and ask prepared questions	I did it and barely had to think about it

What was the MOST difficult part of this challenge? What did we learn?

It is still really hard when anyone acts surprised. We learned that it really does start to feel easier with practice!

**Success with
Important Adults**
*This worksheet helps
organize and track progress
through important but
difficult verbal interactions
with known adults.*

Victory Valley

Celebrating Success!

With Mount Mindful, we illustrated the importance of how small achievements or accomplishments lead to forward momentum and eventually big outcomes. The Victory Valley handout may be used to keep track of your child's major accomplishments. Many parents make fun charts, keep a journal, or create a wall display because tracking achievements (paired with reward charts to track everyday successes) can be especially motivating for many kids.

With each new victory, the child is reminded that they have overcome a situation that made them anxious and fearful. Anxiety's role is to keep us safe by encouraging us to avoid fearful activities. When we face those activities instead, no matter what the outcome, we learn that we are stronger than the fear. This sets off a cascade of momentum for children and may even spread to situations outside of speaking. Celebrate these steps and help your child keep moving forward!

Victory Valley Instruction Handout

Instructions:

Celebrate great achievements in your child's journey to overcome SM by placing the icons (page left) on the next page, *Victory Valley - Celebrate Success Handout*. These icons may be copied, cut out, and pasted onto the handout. The *Victory Valley - Celebrate Success Handout* can be used weekly, monthly, or over a period of several months. You may even choose to use this handout for the journey as a whole. Icons might be earned when a new milestone or goal is reached at school, with peers, in the community, or after demonstrating a new Mount Mindful skill. It will be up to each family if and how to use the handout.

Helpful Hints:

* Victory Valley will not be right for every family. Some children are reluctant to "own" an achievement after the first success.
* This handout is not a reward system in the traditional sense, it is meant to be an intrinsic motivator. A place where children can visually see all (or some) of their important achievements.
* Let your child have fun and make this worksheet their own! Give them ownership and let them take the lead!

My art project wasn't perfect (not exactly how I wanted it) but I didn't let it ruin my day.

Answered a "pop-up" person at post office!

It's been so hard to talk to Aunt Sophie. It took me four tries today but I finally did it. I kept trying & I didn't give up!!

Spoke to Alison for the first time!!

Walked into school ALONE today!!

Completed "Show and Tell" Challenge Pathway!

Said "Thank you" to cashier for the first time!!

Victory Valley
Celebrate Success

It is such a joy to see a recently anxious, inhibited child acting brave and confident, speaking to new adults, and making new friends – any and all gains are to be cherished! While most gains tend to be permanent and lead to forward momentum, some small regressions can occur. Although it is rare for children to regress back to where they were before intervention, it is not uncommon for progress to stall.

Helping a child overcome selective mutism can be quite challenging and even the most well-intentioned parents (and other adults) will need to be cognizant of potential pathway pitfalls:

- **Don't reward without success.** For example, if a child's brave work goal is to order ice cream and, despite practicing and planning, they simply are not able to order, what do you do as a parent? Do you order the ice cream for them so that they are not sad or to pacify the waiting people in line behind them? *No.* Parents can either make the prompt easier or stop the practice exercise and try again another time, saying "I know that you tried hard, and we will try again next time."

    > If your child expects to get ice cream at the parlor, or a piece of cheese at the grocery store, it will seem unfair to suddenly change the rules without warning. Make sure to discuss the new plan with your child, create small and obtainable goals, and be clear about expectations.

For some activities, it might be better to practice a new step when siblings are left at home. It would be very difficult to deny your child with SM ice cream while others are eating. Likewise, everyone missing out on ice cream is not a great situation. If you attempt to tackle the next step while the rest of the family is with you, parents must be very intentional with expectations so that the child will find success and take part in the reward (especially a reward like ice cream!).

- **Don't mind read.** Parents of children with SM may be uniquely attuned to nonverbal cues their child might use to communicate their needs. Kids need for us to reduce our automatic knowledge of what they want, and begin asking them to take responsibility for indicating, even nonverbally, their choices, needs, and desires.

- **Don't be critical or discouraging with your words.** Take great care not to be critical or discouraging, or to say things aloud in front of the child that suggest they are incapable of speaking or carrying through with a task. It is easy for these statements to slip out – when the teacher says that the class will be doing a presentation, the parent blurts out, "Oh, Jack will never be able to do that!" This undermines the child….and kids *believe* what we say!

- **Take great care NOT to allow the child to see your anxiety or frustration**. This is not about *our* goals and where *we* think they should be – it is about **their** goals and **their** progress. Success can take time.

- **Don't provide escape routes or avoidance techniques**. Children with SM may use many tactics to avoid speech as a result of their anxiety. Parents must be aware of these avoidance techniques and work to reduce them. That is not to say that the expectation should immediately be that the child must speak in sentences to get what they want, but that eventually "talking gets the good stuff" (even when talking means one syllable).

- **Don't avoid practicing regularly.** Not practicing brave talking enough leads directly to… not brave talking. The child must practice frequently and repeatedly to be successful and for those gains to be maintained.

- **Don't set the bar too high.** Many adults don't realize that what they are asking of the child is too hard and too complex. They ask the child to say "Hi!" to the teacher. This sounds simple, but requires that the child initiate (harder than responding for some children) in front of a group (harder than in private) with a greeting (usually harder than other social interactions for a child with SM). Take care in the goals you set. Careful and thoughtful planning will help determine appropriate goals.

- **Don't ask open-ended questions, especially at first.** These are typically difficult for children with SM to answer. Instead, try to phrase questions as forced-choice (e.g., "Do you want vanilla or chocolate ice cream?").

- **Don't bombard the child with questions.** Ask a question, wait at least five seconds for the child to respond and if they don't respond, ask the same question again or rephrase the same question.

- **Don't focus on polite words… yet.** Many parents complain that the hardest words for their children to say are polite words such as hi, bye, sorry, thank you, please, and excuse me. Research has not found an answer for this phenomenon, but it is possible that children have "over-practiced" avoiding these words. Parents have attempted over and over to encourage their child to say "Please" or "Thank you" in public, and the child has therefore garnered a lot of practice avoiding saying these phrases. Alternatively, saying these words might feel more intimate or personal. For example, thank you means you have done something for me. Please is asking a favor of someone. I'm sorry implies you have somehow hurt someone else. In the beginning of treatment, parents should not prompt their child to greet new communication partners, say goodbye, or thank them. Parents and children can focus on these at a later point, and until that point, prompting them generally only sets the child up for failure.

- **Don't focus on having your child use proper names when speaking to friends and family.** Children with SM are often hesitant or even unable/unwilling to use proper names, despite knowing the names. Again, this may be due to intimacy expectations (e.g., if I admit to knowing a person's name, then maybe it is harder to continue not speaking). This may need to be a higher-level goal.

- **Avoid demanding extended eye contact.** It is best not to demand that your child make eye contact at first, since many children with SM can become overwhelmed by eye contact (making it more difficult to reach speaking milestones).

* **Don't let your anxiety get in the way.** It is okay for a child to struggle a little, and it has to be okay for them to be a little uncomfortable. As noted before, individual growth does not come as a result of doing only things that are easy and comfortable. Undeniably, there will be times when you feel stressed or anxious during the process of helping your child reach their goals. The more relaxed, matter of fact, and "unflappable" you can be when they struggle, the better. It is hard watching children struggle, but they need to struggle in order to gain confidence and understand that they are strong enough to handle discomfort. Eventually, the uncomfortable feeling will dissipate and your child will begin to believe that they can handle any situation thrown at them!

Although rare, when regressions do occur, many times they cannot be linked to anything specific. Parents, therapists, and the school team should be careful not to blame themselves, but simply make plans to modify the intervention to get progress back on track. First, if the regression can be tracked back to one of the above reasons, or another clear reason, the team should problem-solve how to avoid this regression in the future. Second, we must help the child start again at a reasonable point and feel successful. Goals should revert back to the last step that the child was able to accomplish with only a slight amount of discomfort, and the reward system should reflect this (thus, the expectations are shifted to reflect a slightly easier step/goal and the child is again being rewarded for their brave work). Once the child is reliably accomplishing the easier step, parents and the school should attempt to again move the child to the next step on their "Challenge Pathway".

The Most Common Reasons for Regression and Stalling Include:

* A lack of consistent practice being brave
* A new school year, move to a new school, or a new teacher
* Perceived negative feedback (e.g., the child spoke in class and was reprimanded by the teacher harshly)
* Social stresses (e.g., the child is having negative interactions with peers in the classroom or neighborhood)
* Physical changes (e.g., diet, sleep, hormones, puberty, etc.)
* Changes at home
* Expectations and demands that are out of sync with ability (Pathway Hazards: audience, environment, and speech demand)

Many children with SM will benefit from and make gains with the help of a local therapist, their school and/or parents who are informed and motivated to follow expert advice (and this book), but there are times when the child simply doesn't improve. If this is your situation, we suggest that you put more thought into intensive intervention options or a consultation with a highly regarded SM treating professional (discussed in Chapter 4).

Goal Mapping

Determining Goals - Which situations are challenging for your child?

Use the open space below to list challenging situations that your child faces with peers, at school, and in the community.   Which Mount Mindful skills might be important to explore?

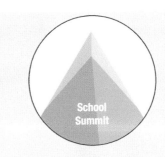

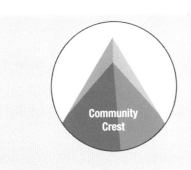

Notes:

Challenge Pathway Planning

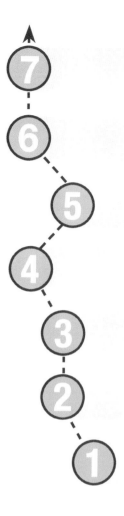

Which factors might influence progress?

THE AUDIENCE

THE ENVIRONMENT

THE SPEECH DEMAND

Notes

Impactful Peer Interactions
Conquering Playdates

Peers

Select peers who are patient, well-liked and helpful (ask the teacher to provide a list if necessary). We recommend beginning with one-on-one interactions. Once the child has conquered one-on-one interactions, small group activities might be next.

Which peer(s) will take part in this interaction and what should they understand prior to the interaction?

Plan

Where will the interaction be?

What will the children be doing?

What will you do to help facilitate?

Outcome & Notes

What worked well? Does anything need to be adjusted for the next interaction? Any breakthroughs?

Preparing for Pop-up People

Instructions: We recommend that this sheet be completed and practiced (as often as possible) before the "Pop-up People Challenge" worksheet. When children are prepared for speaking, interactions will feel easier. This may be a higher level challenge for some children.

Before the challenge

What situations are challenging?	Let's practice what we will say!

After the challenge

We did it! What was the hardest part?

We did it! What did we learn?

Pop-up People Challenge

Instructions: Use this page to track successful interactions with "pop-up people" - unexpected verbal interactions that occur in the community setting. After reaching ten successful verbal interactions, caregivers may choose to provide a special prize!

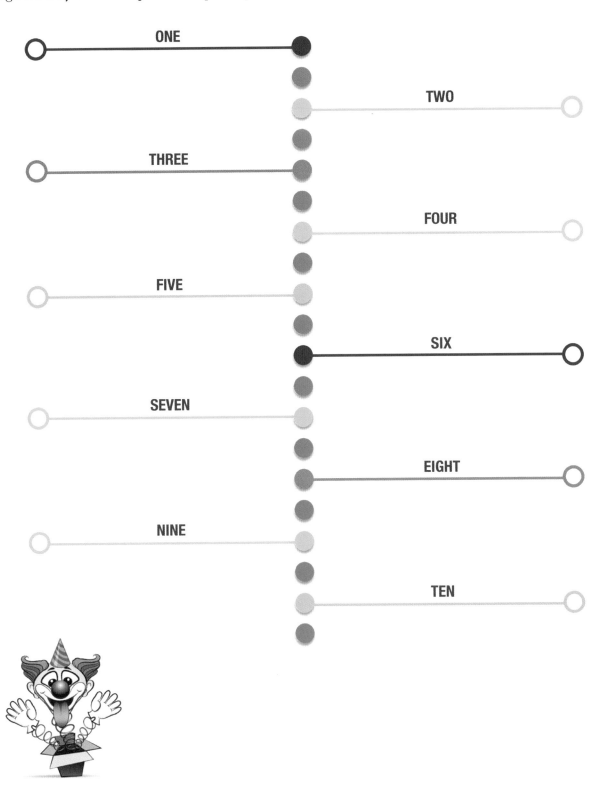

Success with Important Adults

Who are the most challenging people to speak with?

Instructions: Discuss the people with whom your child has difficulty speaking and determine a plan for beginning to speak with these "contaminated" people. Be sure to track and reward successful interactions!

Who	Plan for Speaking	I did it!

What was the MOST difficult part of this challenge? What did we learn?

Person Bingo

Instructions: Use the game cards provided on the next page or get creative in the spaces below. This game will help your child get comfortable asking basic questions of community members with a fun objective. After your child checks off four in a row, you may wish to provide a small prize! Community members might include shopkeepers, patrons, restaurant staff, post office employees, etc.

B **I** **N** **G** **O**

Person Bingo Game Cards

Instructions: The game cards provided here may be written (or cut/pasted) onto the *Person Bingo* worksheet. There are three question sets provided below.

<table>
<tr><td rowspan="12" style="writing-mode: vertical-rl">Bingo Game Card Sets</td></tr>
<tr><td rowspan="4">1</td><td>Find someone who has a sister.</td><td>Find someone who has a pet fish.</td><td>Find someone who has traveled to another country.</td><td>Find someone who likes to take naps.</td></tr>
<tr><td>Find someone whose favorite season is Fall.</td><td>Find someone who likes to play tennis.</td><td>Ask a store clerk if they like the color blue.</td><td>Find someone who has traveled on a train.</td></tr>
<tr><td>Find someone who likes brownies or cake.</td><td>Find someone who has a birthday in March.</td><td>Find someone who has visited the zoo.</td><td>Ask a person with a necklace if they have ever kayaked.</td></tr>
<tr><td>Ask a person with a short haircut if they like to watch TV.</td><td>Find someone who has seen *The Wizard of Oz*.</td><td>Find someone who likes to listen to country music.</td><td>Find a person whose favorite color is green.</td></tr>
<tr><td rowspan="4">2</td><td>Find someone who was born in May.</td><td>Find someone who was has visited New York.</td><td>Ask someone wearing glasses if they like salad.</td><td>Find someone who uses Facebook.</td></tr>
<tr><td>Ask a person with brown hair about their favorite color.</td><td>Find someone who likes strawberries.</td><td>Ask a store clerk how long they have worked at the store.</td><td>Ask someone which holiday is their favorite.</td></tr>
<tr><td>Find someone who has a pet dog.</td><td>Find someone who has a pet cat.</td><td>Find someone in a hat and ask if they like baseball.</td><td>Ask someone where you can find the restroom.</td></tr>
<tr><td>Find someone who likes to ride bikes.</td><td>Find someone who has seen cartoons.</td><td>Find a person who is younger than 30 and ask their age.</td><td>Find someone whose name begins with the letter "A".</td></tr>
<tr><td rowspan="4">3</td><td>Find someone who was born in the Fall.</td><td>Find someone who likes to watch movies.</td><td>Find someone who has a pet hamster/gerbil.</td><td>Ask a store clerk if this is their first job.</td></tr>
<tr><td>Find someone who likes classical music.</td><td>Find someone with blond hair and ask if they have a sister.</td><td>Find someone who likes to drink coffee.</td><td>Find someone who likes to go bowling.</td></tr>
<tr><td>Find someone who has been to college.</td><td>Ask a person wearing a dress if they like spaghetti.</td><td>Find someone who likes to go camping.</td><td>Find someone born in a state that starts with the letter "N".</td></tr>
<tr><td>Find someone whose favorite color is purple or pink.</td><td>Find someone who likes to sew or knit.</td><td>Find someone who has served in the military.</td><td>Find someone whose name starts with the letter "M".</td></tr>
</table>

And the Survey Says...

Instructions: Choose four questions from the *Example Survey Questions* (next page) that your child can ask to 10 adults and/or children. When appropriate, caregivers may choose to offer a prize (perhaps only after one or two interactions or when the survey is complete, depending on skill level).

Survey Questions				
1				
2				
3				
4				
5				
6				
7				
8				
9				
10				

Participant Responses

Example Survey Questions

Instructions: The questions provided here may be written (or cut/pasted) onto the *And the Survey Says…* worksheet.

Survey Question Sets				
1	What is your favorite food?	Do you like cookies or cake better?	What is your favorite candy?	Do you like water, milk, or juice better?
2	What is your favorite movie?	What is your favorite song?	Do you like to watch cartoons?	What is your favorite book to read?
3	What is your favorite kind of ice cream?	Do you like sprinkles, nuts or candy on top?	Do you like fudge, caramel or no sauce on top?	Where is your favorite place to get ice cream?
4	What is your name?	How many siblings do you have?	In what state were you born?	In what month were you born?
5	What is your favorite sport?	Do you play any sports?	Do you have a favorite team?	Who is your favorite player?
6	Where do you like to travel?	Do you prefer to travel by car or plane?	Do you like cold places or warm places?	What is your favorite souvenir from your travels?
7	What is your favorite animal?	Do you have any pets?	Do you like big dogs or small dogs better?	What is the scariest animal or insect you have touched?
8	What is your favorite color?	Do you like to take photographs?	Do you have a favorite piece of art?	Have you ever made a sculpture out of clay?
9	What is your favorite state?	Have you been to any other countries?	To which country would you most like to travel?	Which country has the best food?
10	What is your favorite subject in school?	Do you bring your lunch or eat from the cafeteria?	Who is your favorite teacher?	Which country has the best food?
11	Can you name a type of snake?	Can you name a type of shark?	Can you name a type of ant?	Can you name a type of bird?
12	What do you like best about the outdoors?	Do you like to go camping?	Have you ever been swimming in a lake?	Do you like to go bike riding?

Brave Work Log

Instructions: The Brave Work Log is a place to track every attempt by the child to meet a specific challenge or goal at school, therapy, home, etc. This log may be passed back and forth between parents and members of the child's care team, OR each party responsible for intervention activities may have a separate copy of this log sheet.

DATE	Challenge/Step	Notes/Comments	Audience Who was involved?	Environment Where did the intervention happen?	Speech Demand How did the child interact?

Chapter Eight

THE REST OF ANNA'S JOURNEY

Beginning Specialized Selective Mutism Treatment ("Intensive Treatment")

Over the summer before Anna started Kindergarten and in the early fall, I began to put more thought and study into selective mutism. During my research I came across information about "intensive treatment." I learned that intensive treatment allows children with SM to participate in an extended and concentrated dose of exposure therapy and that there are various "centers for excellence" around the country where clinicians work with children regularly. We zeroed in on a program that we thought would be a good fit. In October, we packed our van for a family road trip hoping, at the very least, to find some answers and praying for a minor miracle.

We did not find the miracle for which we had hoped. It was discouraging to learn that a program which helps so many was not able to help our family. If the experts couldn't help us, we wondered who could? For many children and families, these programs are life changing but when we returned home, we discovered that Anna had regressed in some ways. She seemed even more anxious about certain situations and began to withhold speech from us in the community.

We gently reminded Anna that she does, in fact, speak with us in public and we would like for her to practice doing so. The next day, we had fun rewarding her with a check mark for each time she spoke with us at a restaurant. She earned several (easy) checks and got to pick a prize. After we had Anna somewhat back to "baseline," we let her know that we planned to continue working with her to use her voice. We assured her that we would go more slowly and hopefully it would feel easier. After that conversation, Andrew and I needed to be BRAVE when we tried to practice ordering ice cream (especially when Anna fell to the floor and had a massive tantrum because we suggested that she try and say "vanilla"). It was obvious that no reward would help her over the hump of ordering by herself. We didn't want to do any more "damage" so we stopped practicing while we began to think about our plans going forward.

Fortunately, I was already scheduled to attend the Selective Mutism Association's annual conference. It was an opportunity to learn more about SM, meet the leading professionals treating

SM, and help determine next steps for Anna. I had so many questions and I was determined to speak with as many experts as I possibly could. By the end of the conference, I had picked up important insight and ideas that helped us to formulate a plan for Anna.

It became clear that we were going to need a knowledgeable guide, an expert in treating SM, to coach our team back home through the steps necessary to get Anna speaking. Ultimately, I researched several options and we decided to begin conversations with Dr. Kotrba in Michigan and Dr. Fernald, a speech language pathologist in Florida. Dr. Fernald happens to be located near my parent's home and she was able to fit us in for a consultation during a visit.

Dr. Fernald follows the DIR/Floortime® model which integrates social emotional development, individual differences (sensory processing, speech/language skills, visual spatial skills, and motor planning) and building relationships as part of an interdisciplinary framework for intervention. It involves following the child's lead and engaging the child on their level, while moving the child up the developmental ladder. We arrived to find an "indoor playground" similar to the OT clinic that Anna was accustomed to attending every week. She was very much at home on the therapy equipment (swing, trampoline, and toys) and she quickly jumped right into playing and having a good time. Once ready, Dr. Fernald had Anna stand inside of a small tent and wait to receive a big exercise ball that was being rolled into the tent. Dr. Fernald was focused on helping Anna initiate communication. She told Anna to click her tongue when she was ready for Dr. Fernald to roll the ball into the tent. The brilliance of that particular activity was that Anna was shielded from view and perhaps she felt a little more confident in using her voice by reducing visual stimuli. Dr. Fernald had progressed Anna in a short time to making sounds which are then shaped into words.

Later, we connected with Dr. Kotrba by phone to learn more about her treatment methodology. We spoke at length about Anna's history and about our desire to move things along slowly. We explained that we needed an expert on our team to help establish a plan for Anna as well as provide on-going support and guidance. We ended the call with a great feeling about Dr. Kotrba's behavioral treatment approach.

In January, Anna, Nana, and I began our drive to Michigan to meet with Dr. Kotrba. We told Anna that just like there are a lot of children that are challenged with talking, there are a lot of doctors that help those children. We told her that every doctor is different, just like every little girl and boy is different, and that we would try and have more fun with this doctor. Our approach from the very beginning of this trip was entirely different than our first trip.

When we arrived at the hotel in Michigan, we were thrilled to find a fantastic indoor pool. After we settled in, I told Anna that we could go swimming. The water was cold and I really did NOT want to go in. It would require me to be super brave because I HATE cold water (a fact that Anna knows well). I told her that we could swim every day and that I'd do something brave if she tried to be

138 Overcoming Selective Mutism

brave with Dr. K. every day. Anna said that to be really brave, I would need to jump into the deep end and scream "poopy face." I was happy to oblige, with the understanding that this was a quid pro quo agreement (and we were the only people in the pool). This went on for a while; she had me jumping into the pool every which way and saying all kinds of crazy stuff. She loved it!

Determined to find success and carve out a path forward for Anna, I put a lot of thought into the small details. We brought beanie boos (stuffed animals) to play with, a Lego friend's house to build, stickers and we also brought Shopkins™. Shopkins™ are tiny, tiny collectible plastic figures based on grocery store items. I had avoided caving to this trendy collectible but Anna wanted them (she wanted them badly). Knowing that rewards, if used correctly, can be game changing for children with SM, I gave in and ordered several packages of Shopkins™, resigning myself to the inevitably of finding these tiny figures all over my house (for years to come).

While we drove to Dr. Kotrba's office for the first day of intensive treatment, I tried to keep the mood in the car light and airy. I reminded Anna that I was brave in the pool and that I bet she could be brave today. If she was brave, I would also be brave in the pool later in the day. I verbally reenacted the pool scene from the day before including all of the wild words she made me say. With each utterance of each wacky word, she relaxed and laughed all over again! The mood was set and it was silly!

Due to an unexpected emergency, Dr. Kotrba's colleague, Katelyn Reed, stepped in for the first day of intensive therapy. I was a little anxious about starting the first day without Dr. K., but as it turned out I had nothing to be worried about. Only minutes after we arrived, it was clear that Katelyn knew what she was doing. Katelyn was very relaxed and natural, she had a great calmness about her. She clearly understood the nuances of working with children with SM. Anna had severe separation anxiety and it would have felt traumatic for her (and therefore she would not have spoken) if I left the room, so I remained with her for the duration. While Anna would not respond verbally to Katelyn at first, she was willing to play a game with us. She shook her head yes or no, and by the end of the first day, she was making sounds with Katelyn. Her sticker sheet was almost full, she felt successful, and she was able to select several Shopkins™ as rewards. Anna was tired but she was still excited for our evening swim and she was still willing to play the "brave" game.

The next day, we met with Dr. K. and I was so relieved that she was able to pick up where Katelyn left off. Of course, she is also a natural working with children who are learning bravery and overcoming SM. Dr. K is truly an expert, blending many of the latest research-based techniques for SM. She was calm and reassuring while progressing Anna toward speech through shaping (tool #4). One of the first things that she did was to work with Anna on blowing air through her lips. They do a fantastic exercise with cotton balls where they literally race them on a table by blowing air with their mouths. For children who are struggling and can't seem to speak at all, even blowing air can be challenging. However, for many children, it is attainable and it can be a "gateway" as it was for Anna. She progressed to beginning sounds and then we worked on first sounds, end sounds, and then combining them to make "yes" and "no." For the rest of the second day, and the next day, we also worked on stimulus fading (tool #3) with other staff members. They were experts at fading into our games and activities and they helped Anna to hone her ability to produce short answers when prompted. At times it was slow and tedious, but we were finding success by the third day in the form of simple responses to easy questions.

After Intensive Therapy

Intensive therapy is just the beginning. It is NOT magic for most kids. And it wasn't magic for Anna. While for some kids it does seem to work to move them past their fear of speaking very quickly, for MOST kids it is more of a springboard toward reaching their goals. Intensive therapy is a time of learning for all involved. Caregivers learn how to work with their children when they return home. Teachers (usually by video or phone conference) are given instructions on how to modify their interactions with the child. Even the clinician will be taking notes and jotting down ideas to identify the best way to assist the family back home. Adults must be supportive and determined to "generalize" the gains after intensive treatment (by practicing the skills frequently with new people, in new locations, and with new demands). It is also important to find someone locally to guide your team and/or to stay in touch with the clinician who conducted the intensive intervention (by phone if necessary) to help with continued progress.

New Brave Talking Partners
Anna used this handout to track her successes in talking to new peers; as we filled in the circles she felt increasingly accomplished!

Community Exposure

Practice makes proficient when it comes to SM. I felt compelled to keep Anna and myself on track and to make sure that we were accountable for our practice. Most people who know me would probably think that I'm organized but I never, ever, FEEL organized. When I begin something new, I usually have a strong NEED to feel organized. Community exposure, for Anna, was no exception and so I channeled my years of experience with PowerPoint and Excel as a management consultant. I enjoyed creating helpful charts and worksheets to motivate Anna and assist us in reaching our goals. I began creating worksheets for the situation at hand and our first worksheet helped guide us toward adding new speaking partners. The example provided on the next page is Anna's completed worksheet with her artwork.

New Brave Talking Partners *Example*

Instructions: Each circle represents a new speaking partner. Write the name and color in the circle to match the person you spoke with!

The fearless are merely fearless.

People who ACT in spite of their fear are TRULY BRAVE!

I told Anna that when we added ten new speaking partners she would get a big prize - a fun day around town to celebrate! Because Anna loves art, I thought it would be fun for her to draw each new partner out of the circles on the worksheet page. We started with my friend Lisa. Anna didn't know Lisa well but Lisa knew all about Anna and she was prepared for our afternoon. She was a sympathetic, patient and "safe" person.

We started with cotton ball races and then moved on to sounds, using shaping techniques (tool #4). Anna eventually answered questions, but never moved into a more natural speaking flow with Lisa despite a couple of more meetings. After Lisa, we had a new babysitter and Anna didn't want to use the shaping steps with her. She told me that she could talk to Mary without the shaping steps. Sure enough, Anna did it! After Mary, we were able to add several more talking partners slowly throughout the spring.

In addition to "new" adults in our home, we began working right away on community members – shopkeepers, restaurant waitstaff, library workers, etc. We started with first sounds and we worked our way up to asking pre-determined questions. We did not use polite words or greetings like "excuse me", "hi", "please" or "thank you". Those were too hard for Anna. I started the interaction by introducing Anna and then I would say, "We are working on brave talking today, would you mind if we ask you a few questions?". In the year that we were doing this type of practice, I only had one person say no! We had a few that didn't seem to have patience but honestly most people were so happy to help and even thought that what we were doing was fantastic. I never went into detail about SM, just that we were working on being brave and talking with new people. In addition to speaking goals, we had goals such as eye contact and "giving and taking." Anna had to practice giving money to cashiers and taking items such as the cookie or ice cream that she ordered directly from the server. Kids with SM tend to have difficulty with these types of exchanges, even if they don't require speech, and so it is important to give them opportunities to practice. Giving movie tickets to the usher, grabbing the bag from the store cashier, and handing over money to pay for items are all good options for practice.

To keep Anna motivated, almost every outing ended with ice cream that she had to order (in whichever way she was currently able). In the beginning, it was with first sounds. Anna would say, "I" for ice cream. That was it! With our new and slower mindset, we were able to avoid meltdowns on the floor of the ice cream parlor. Saying "I", in a whisper, was achievable for Anna and we slowly progressed to more sounds and finally to simply saying "ice cream." Because the toy store was right next to the ice cream parlor, many days we made our way over there too. At the time, Anna was highly motivated to add to her Beanie Boo™ stuffed animal collection and so we capitalized on her enthusiasm. The manager of the toy store was especially amazing with Anna. She learned how to communicate with Anna by limiting speaking demands in the beginning and then eventually asking "forced-choice" questions (providing the answer choices as part of the question such as, "Do you want the purple Beanie Boo or the pink one?").

During the late spring, approximately six months after the intensive in Michigan, we had a week of major accomplishments! Of all places, it started with the dentist even though Anna had a history of "over-reacting" during dental appointments. Prior to the cleaning, Anna and I decided that she would try and be brave and answer questions from the hygienist. The hygienist spoke to Anna with no expectation and then as time went by, she peppered in a few questions. When this happened, I tried to slow things down to give Anna time to speak. If needed, I repeated the question, queuing Anna that an answer was expected. Anna answered with a whisper! After the appointment, the hygienist enthusiastically but privately noted Anna's progress!

The next day, I took Anna to an art festival. When we arrived, Anna made a beeline for the face painter. As we waited in line, I told her that she should tell the painter what she wanted. We practiced a few times and despite some hesitation, Anna did it! She asked in a soft whisper to get a butterfly painted on her arm! We started to make great progress when Anna's friends began to join us for our adventures. We really stepped up our game, bringing along a clipboard with surveys and games that involved speaking with mall patrons and workers (see worksheets in chapter 7). The clipboard was an excellent prop! The kids passed the clipboard back and forth and took turns filling in the worksheets. They felt official! We progressed to including more socially appropriate language including "hi", "please" and "thank you." "Excuse me" was the hardest for Anna but eventually she was able to do it. Having her friends along made her braver and she was able to model some of their more natural speaking patterns!

Anna still struggled with "pop-up people." As we discussed in the previous chapter, when people appear or pop up out of nowhere and start asking questions (with no time for preparation) children can find it difficult to respond. I coined the term "pop-up people" because Anna's reaction was always to freeze, as if she was stunned by a "jack in the box" toy when the top pops open! From the overly friendly person at the store who wants to inquire about age, grade, or her favorite princess, to the check-out person who asks about her hair and probes for her name, to the mom at the park who is interested in which school she attends, pop-up people were lurking everywhere! We needed to intentionally focus on these situations, so I created a series of worksheets (see chapter 7) and we went to work. Advanced preparation and practice helped Anna to finally conquer these types of encounters. In the moment, if it was needed, I would repeat the question and that allowed Anna to feel as though she was answering me. It also gave her extra time to think through her answer.

Preparing for Pop-Up People and Pop-Up People Challenge Worksheets
Available at the end of Chapter 7.

Full Voice Fish Bowl Challenge
This worksheet can provide ideas for slow practices to encourage full voice verbalizations in the community setting or to encourage progress toward another goal.

No matter how comfortable Anna was becoming with answering and asking questions, it was always in a whisper. We needed to make a concerted effort to move her into her full voice. As always, we discussed it and we decided it was time to work on voice volume. At the time, Anna was very excited about getting a pet fish. We came up with a special worksheet called the "Full Voice Fish Bowl Challenge" like the one seen here. When Anna successfully used her FULL voice ten times, she would earn a fish. For Anna the key has always been setting a goal, deciding on an appropriate and motivating reward, practicing, and then executing. The reward needed to feel immediately tangible at the very beginning of a new challenge. Having a friend along was also very motivating for Anna and increased our odds of success. Even though Anna didn't get a fish on our first visit to the pet store, she was able to pick out a fish bowl and the rock. The next time we went, she picked up the sea plant and statue, and then finally on the third time, she got a lovely Beta fish that she named "Starfire Lizzy."

When working with your child to move from a whisper to a fuller voice, the following phrases might help: "Say it a little louder.", "I don't think they could hear you.", "Could you hear her?", "What was that, Jack?"

"Full Voice" Fish Bowl Challenge *Example*

Instructions: Use the spaces below to document each instance of brave work and then place a check near one fishbowl item. This challenge works well at the pet store or anywhere in the community at large. Prizes might be the tangible items listed below and earned right away or at the end of the challenge.

	Brave Work Practice		
1	*8/17/18 : At Pet store, used full voice for first syllable "W"*	**7**	*9/10/18 : At Pet store, used full voice for first three words "Where is the"*
2	*8/20/18 : Used full voice for the first syllable "W"*	**8**	*9/13/18 : Used full voice for the first three words "Where is the"*
3	*8/23/18: Used full voice for the first first word "Where"*	**9**	*9/18/18: At pet store, used full voice for entire sentence, "Where is the fish food?"*
4	*8/27/18: Used full voice for the first first word "Where"*	**10**	*9/18/18: Used full voice for entire sentence, "Where is the fish net?"*
5	*8/30/18: At pet store, used full voice for the first two words "Where is"*	**11**	*9/18/18: Used full voice for entire sentence, "Where are the fish bowls?"*
6	*9/4/18: Used full voice for the first two words "Where is"*	**12**	*9/18/18: Used full voice for entire sentence, "Where is the restroom?"*

☑ **Fish Bowl**   ☑ **Statue #1**
☑ **Rock**   ☑ **Statue #2**
☑ **Plant #1**   ☑ **Fish Food**
☑ **Plant #2**   ☑ **Fish Net**
☑ **Plant #3**   ☑ **FISH!!!!**

Beginning to speak in a "contaminated environment" is one of the most difficult situations for a child with SM to overcome. "Contamination" can be so challenging that even after intensive treatment or consistent weekly therapy, with improvements made outside of the school setting, silence can still exist within the walls of the school. Anecdotally, many parents have reported that moving to a new school can be helpful. It gives the child a fresh start where they are no longer known as "the kid who does not talk." Of course, depending on the child's age and maturity level, you may wish to include them in the decision-making process.

Success with Important Adults Available at the end of Chapter 7.

We approached speaking in a full voice a lot like we first approached speaking (in what turned out to be a whisper) in the beginning. Anna would need to ease into using her more confident voice. She simply wasn't going to begin speaking in a full voice if we didn't break down the steps. Anna was to begin, with one sound or word, in a full voice and then her friend Jordan could jump in and they could ask the rest of the question together. Anna might say, "H" in a full voice and then Jordan and Anna would finish the rest of the sentence together with, "ow old is your dog?" We slowly ramped up to one word in a full voice alone and then more than one word. We often had to remind Anna to raise her voice volume.

Contaminated Environments and People

One of our most difficult tasks was helping Anna to speak with "contaminated" adults. Neighbors, teachers, coaches, and other adults with whom Anna had a history of not speaking required a special plan. Our first step was to remind Anna that we noticed she seemed to have difficulty with some people more than others. Eventually we created a list of neighbors and other contaminated people that we would work through one-by-one. This required some preparation on my part, as I had to contact each person, plan a get-together and coach them on how to increase our chances of success. A large part of the "coaching" involved passing along information on child directed and verbal directed interaction (tools #1 and #2) and using forced choice questions. Essentially, I was asking our friends NOT to ask questions in the beginning, be relaxed (and silly if possible), use forced-choice questions, allow extra time for an answer, repeat the question if needed, and not to react or make a big deal when she speaks.

Our first get together was with our neighbors, Gerry and Mark. Jordan, their daughter, and Anna played together often and Anna was frequently at their house but was in the habit of shaking her head to answer or whispering her answers to Jordan. We planned a game night to include games that I knew would encourage speech. Our games were home-made and we used them quite frequently at school as well. The great thing about these games is that kids love them and each turn requires speech! When Anna and I brought our games across the street, everyone knew what to do! Anna knew that she was going to use her voice with Gerry and Mark. I would be guiding the activities and Gerry and Mark were reminded to follow the "ground rules." Most importantly, we had fun.

"Question" Jenga™ was the first game we played and requires that each Jenga™ block contain a question (handwritten, in advance). When a block is pulled out from the Jenga™ tower, there are several options for incorporating speech. During our game, I was the designated question reader for Anna's first several turns. I asked the questions and she answered. For the later rounds, Gerry was the question reader and Anna answered! We played several more rounds and Mark also had a turn as the question reader. Success!

Our next "game" was modified from occupational therapy and involves using a set of kid friendly "tweezers" to find small animals hidden in a box of dry beans. Kids of all ages (and adults too) LOVE the hidden animals game! There must be something about the surprise and novelty of digging through dry beans with tweezers and discovering a hidden creature. Again, this game can be played various ways to incorporate speech. We decided that Jordan and Anna would take turns digging for animals and that the parents, would take turns asking questions about the animal that was uncovered. When Anna "unearthed" a shark, we took turns asking basic questions such as, "Where does a shark live?". Anna was completely verbal during the hidden animals game.

After the smashing success of game night, Anna was "primed" for speech but Gerry still had to use some advanced skills to solidify speech with Anna. I remember Gerry telling me how hard it was and that she really had to "insist" on speech in some cases. She used a lot of forced choice questions and eventually Anna became completely natural in her speech with Gerry and Mark! One by one, we worked through our list of other contaminated people and places.

School Work

For many children with SM (Anna included), school is the MOST contaminated and the most difficult environment to move from silence to speech. Teachers and staff in the educational setting are essential to the success of children working to overcome SM and I am so grateful to all of Anna's teachers who went above and beyond!

Anna returned to school in mid-January, after attending Dr. Kotrba's intensive therapy in Michigan, with a new plan. We needed to systematically expose Anna to speaking at school. At the beginning, it was important that we planned exposures outside of her classroom, but still in the school. By the middle of the school year, her history of not speaking in the classroom meant that we were likely to have better success in a different setting. The resource room was available and we started there one day a week. On those days, we did not do community exposures. We worked on brave talking in the community and in the school simultaneously, but we did so in a way that would not overwhelm Anna.

For the first school exposure, post-intensive, we chose to keep things simple. We met with Mrs. Morris (Anna's Kindergarten teacher) in the resource room and we had a classmate join us. Our goal was to help Anna make any form of progress toward speech with Mrs. Morris. Anna has always accomplished more with friends along for support so I brought games that were fun for all and everyone got stickers, checkmarks, and a small prize for their efforts – I didn't want Anna to feel singled out or as if she was being treated differently and I didn't want her friends to feel as if they were being left out. Mrs. Morris helped to select the student that would join us each week. I brought several game options in case my

It is helpful to let friends, neighbors, teachers, extended family, etc. know that they may feel uncomfortable when they are using speech promoting tools such as verbal directed interaction with forced choice questions. It may feel as if they are "insisting" on speech and it may feel odd and "pushy." It is natural to feel uncomfortable during the process. In fact, it's to be expected. Remember to go slow and allow for extra time! Please note that we are not advocating for an aggressive or forceful encounter but rather an assertive encounter, one that allows the child extra time to answer and communicates (without words) that an answer is expected.

While some children are able to speak in a single session of stimulus fading, other children may require several sessions of stimulus fading before they are able to speak. Remember that each child will move at their own pace.

first choice didn't work. We needed to string together several positive outcomes in order to get Anna comfortable speaking at school.

Through stimulus fading practices (tool #3), Anna was able to speak in a whisper directly to Mrs. Morris in the resource room. As she became more natural with her speech in the resource room, we changed our meeting location to a corner of the classroom. We still invited a friend to help and we still played games. The only factor that changed was the environment. Success! At long last, near the end of the school year Anna finally spoke to Mrs. Morris in her classroom!

Anna Speaking with Her Teacher at School, in the Classroom

Challenge Pathway Example

Speaking to the teacher in the classroom with planned practice – teacher only asks questions that Anna is prepared to answer, teacher leads (several weeks) **4**

Speaking with the teacher in a corner of the classroom – continue stimulus fading, only changing the environment to the corner of classroom (the audience and the speech demand remained consistent), mom leads (two weeks) **3**

Speaking naturally to the teacher in a resource room – play games with teacher and a friend using stimulus fading techniques (tool #4) three times per week, mom leads (several weeks) **2**

Working toward speech with the teacher in a resource room – play games with teacher and friend using shaping techniques (tool #4) once per week, mom leads (time frame: several weeks) **1**

Moving to Montessori for First Grade

We are fortunate that our school district has a public Montessori option (1st – 8th grade). After discussing the pros and cons of Montessori education with Dr. Kotrba, I scheduled a meeting with the principal. Jody Swanigan (Ms. Jody) took a profound interest in understanding Anna's special needs, answering my questions and helping to craft a plan for Anna's transition to Montessori. Because Ms. Jody has a daughter the same age as Anna, she offered to meet us for playdates so Anna would get to know her outside of the school environment. Anna was just beginning to speak with a few new adults so Ms. Jody and I worked in tandem with verbal directed interaction (tool #2) to elicit speech. Many times, I repeated Ms. Jody's questions and Anna directed the answer to me.

The guidance and preparation offered by Ms. Jody and the staff helped to kick off Anna's first grade school year moving in a positive direction.

- **Montessori after-school art class:** At our very first meeting in the spring before Anna started at Montessori, Ms. Jody suggested that we register Anna for an after-school art class that was about to begin and run through the end of the school year. Ms. Eliza, the art teacher, agreed to talk with me before the first day and we reviewed information about SM and what Ms. Eliza could do to help. I also asked if I could attend the class with Anna. For the first time, Anna was verbal in a classroom from the beginning! Ms. Eliza used forced choice questions and Anna answered them in a whisper. If Anna needed additional supplies, I coached her on what to say to Ms. Eliza. We created a school environment where speech was expected and established prior to school starting!

- **Visitation day:** At the end of the school year, new students are invited to spend a morning with the lower elementary teachers (even if they don't currently attend Montessori). Ms. Jody casually suggested that we may wish for Anna to skip this event. She felt like it might be too chaotic for Anna. I was reluctant for Anna to miss the event but I knew that it would be impossible to effectively manage the morning to ensure that we were not "contaminating" the new school or any of the teachers.

- **Montessori Institute:** During the summer, new students attend "Montessori Institute," a chance for them to learn about the school and get comfortable with the differences they might expect at Montessori. Ms. Jody set us up to meet with the institute teachers early in the summer and Anna had a chance to play games and approach speaking with them in a way that felt comfortable before Institute week. I prepared them by reviewing the handouts about SM we provide in this book and I left them with additional information about Anna. Institute week went well - Anna spoke with the new teachers in a whisper!

- **The quiet entrance:** Ms. Jody mentioned that part of the Montessori philosophy is a celebration of the first day of school and so, on the first day, the teachers and staff get loud and silly and greet students rather wildly on their way into the school. She assumed that this probably wouldn't be optimal for Anna. In fact, not only did she provide a "quiet entrance" option for Anna but she extended that option to any other student that might feel more comfortable with a less boisterous start to school.

* **Meeting Anna's 1ˢᵗ grade teachers**: We arranged two meetings with her new teachers, Ms. Virginia and Ms. Ali, during the week before school started. The first meeting went well; we played games and Anna spoke in a whisper with both teachers. During the second meeting, remarkably, Anna gave a book report! Students at the Montessori are expected to read a book over the summer and bring in props to help them discuss the book with their classmates. The chances of Anna being able to accomplish this task within the first few days of school were slim, but I didn't want Anna to be excused from the assignment. She read an American Girl Doll book and we brought some of the items that came with the book to help with the discussion. Anna was excited to share and she did amazingly well. She spoke (in a whisper) about the book and answered questions. What progress from only a year prior!

Knowing potential pitfalls is so important and I am truly grateful to Ms. Jody for so masterfully guiding us into a wonderful start of the year and setting us on a positive (verbal) course. Even with momentum on our side, Anna spent most of 1ˢᵗ grade whispering with her teachers. When they asked her to speak up or prompted her for a louder voice, they reported that she appeared as if she would cry. They feared a setback if they pushed her and we decided to let her get comfortable speaking with them first before pushing for a louder, fuller voice. Although Anna was verbal with some of her specials teachers, she was not able to speak with most other teachers and parent volunteers just yet.

Eventually, we needed to work on being brave and raising her voice volume so that her teachers could better hear her. After winter break, we decided to put some concerted effort into moving Anna beyond the whisper. Much like before with her kindergarten teacher, we started outside of the classroom with games, rewards, and gentle expectation. It worked again this time and, after several weeks of work, Anna was speaking in a full voice with Mrs. Virginia and Mrs. Ali. In addition to our work with her classroom teachers, we also began to do school-wide "surveys" and "scavenger hunts" with many of the teachers and staff so that she was practicing using her full voice at school more often. It wasn't long before she began speaking in a full voice to most staff members.

First grade ended with tremendous growth for Anna. She participated in a stage performance with other students where she whispered two lines (and laughed and smiled) while performing dance numbers. She also dressed up as Princess Diana and delivered lines telling onlookers about her character at "wax museum" day (louder than a whisper but quieter than a full voice!). At the very end of the year, she had to create a biome project and answer questions about the animal she selected. She became quite an expert on the seahorse and although she wanted me by her side, she nervously answered questions as other parents made their way around the room. It was an exciting year!

Anna is a happy and confident 2nd grader. She worked so hard to overcome SM and she is a confident speaker in almost every situation. Anna helps other children practice "brave talking" when she can and she is so proud that she can help. Anna often chooses to speak in situations even if they do not require speech - she will volunteer information and even advocate for herself at times. Our goal is for Anna to become even more comfortable and confident at school and to accomplish confident conversation whenever she wishes. Anna bravely participated in wax museum day, science night, and performed a song and dance with friends in her school talent show this year all while using a nice full and brave voice! We are almost at the end of our journey with SM and we could not be more proud of Anna for her bravery and courage in overcoming this very unique challenge.

I "interviewed" Anna recently with the intention of helping her to write a short story about her journey with "brave talking." Together, Anna and I used that conversation to weave together her thoughts on moving past silence.

In her words...

My name is Anna and when I was little, it was very hard and scary to talk. I didn't trust people. I felt embarrassed and worried; sometimes at school I felt like screaming and running away, but I never did. There was one kid who said mean things to me, but I couldn't tell anyone, and it made me feel mad.

The biggest thing that I learned about "brave talking" is that I will feel scared but I still have to get through it. I had to learn to be brave with a lot of things, not just talking. We practiced bravery with trying new foods, school drop off, walking in the hallways at school by myself, and trying new things. I learned to push through my scared feelings, let it happen and then I would feel better.

Now, I don't have trouble talking to people. I don't feel scared anymore but sometimes I still have trouble telling people how I feel. When I meet new people, I don't feel scared anymore! I am not shy at all and I'm kind of outgoing. If you are a kid reading this, I bet you need help brave talking too! Don't be embarrassed or worried at all. I was just like you and I have met other kids just like us. They are brave too! You can do it!!! Just remember - it won't always feel so scary.

I want to give some "shout-outs" to some people who helped me:

☀ *My Mom – She helped me so much and I always felt warm and cozy and relaxed when my mom would help me. (Mom here – I SWEAR she said this!)*

☀ *Emilie and Daddy – They made me laugh and supported me every second of the way.*

☀ *Dr. Kotrba, Katelyn Reed, and the Thriving Minds Team – I am so happy that they knew how to help me and understood me!*

☀ *My teachers and my school – I LOVE my school(s) so much and everyone there really helped me because they were very patient with me.*

☀ *All my family and friends but especially Nana, Summer, Jordan, and Otto – They helped me with brave talking practice at the mall a lot and they also helped me to get my mind off brave talking sometimes.*

Bye, Chow, Shalom, Ta ta, Adios,

Anna, age 8

NEW Brave Talking Partners

Instructions: Each circle represents a new speaking partner. Write the name and color in the circle to match the person you spoke with!

The fearless are merely fearless.

People who ACT in spite of their fear are TRULY BRAVE!

Fish Bowl Challenge

Instructions: Use the spaces below to document each instance of brave work and then place a check near one fishbowl item. This challenge works well at the pet store or anywhere in the community at large. Prizes might be the tangible items listed below and earned right away or at the end of the challenge.

	Brave Work Practice		
1		7	
2		8	
3		9	
4		10	
5		11	
6		12	

❑ Fish Bowl ❑ Statue #1
❑ Rock ❑ Statue #2
❑ Plant #1 ❑ Fish Food
❑ Plant #2 ❑ Fish Net
❑ Plant #3 ❑ FISH!!!!

Chapter Nine

ADDRESSING RELATED CONCERNS

Very few diagnoses of SM are "clean," or without other co-existing challenges. Other diagnoses may also occur alongside selective mutism, including social anxiety disorder, speech and language weaknesses, autism spectrum disorders, and separation anxiety. We provide a brief analysis of these diagnoses and interventions because it is helpful to understand the red flags, tips for intervening, and where to find more help.

Understanding and Intervening with Social Anxiety

Social anxiety (also commonly referred to as social phobia) is highly related to SM; in fact, approximately 90% of kids with SM will also be diagnosed with social anxiety (Dummit E. K., 1997; Kristensen, 2001). Social Anxiety is the persistent fear or anxiety about social situations where one may be scrutinized or judged, or where embarrassing or humiliating situations could occur. This fear may lead to avoidance of social situations. It is easy to see how a fear of speaking could also be related to or grow into a fear of being the center of attention. Children with both selective mutism and social anxiety present with the fear of speaking or communicating, but also may have a fear of being the center of attention (even if not speaking), a fear of others looking at them/watching them, difficulty being in photographs or videos, performance anxiety, and difficulty eating or using the restroom in public. They may avoid situations where others will notice or attend to them, even if no communication is required, and may actively avoid those situations (e.g., refusing to be in sports or extracurriculars, not attending birthday parties, running, hiding, or disengaging when group work is requested by the teacher, etc.). Alternatively, they may attend situations with possible social interactions but still avoid those interactions by sending others nonverbal messages not to engage with them (e.g., not making eye contact, wearing a hoodie or hair over their face, standing in the back of the room, irritated facial expression, etc.).

The evidence-based treatment for social anxiety is quite similar to SM, and frequently involves either behavioral or cognitive-behavioral treatment as well as medication. Children and adolescents are taught to face their fears in a step-wise process (similar to many of the step-wise "challenge pathways" described in this book), first practicing social activities that may be somewhat easier and then moving toward more difficult and anxiety-provoking situations. An example challenge pathway for social anxiety might include:

Playing in a Baseball Game
Challenge Pathway Example

Child goes up to bat independently at a game.

Child practices independently.

Parent starts practice on the field with child for the first 10 minutes, but then child independently practices.

Attends and participates in practice with parent on field, but practices independently fo the last 10 minutes

Participants in practice with parent on the field.

Arrives early to kick the ball with the coach and parent, then stands near the field during practice with parent.

Stands near the field and watches during practice with parent.

The approach for intervening with social anxiety is very similar to the step-wise approach we recommend for overcoming many of the challenges inherit to selective mutism. The child is encouraged by your words (through prompting and possibly with rewards) to face situations that are somewhat anxiety-provoking but manageable, with the understanding that we are often afraid when we are faced with a new situation. We need to be detectives to figure out if the situation REALLY IS scary or if it's just our brain giving us an unhelpful warning signal. Is our guard dog over-reacting again? Are we in danger or are we feeling discomfort? Once they have been successful several times at a specific step on their challenge pathway, the child and parent can work together to take another small step toward being brave in social situations.

Some ideas for social anxiety brave practices include raising a hand to show knowledge in class, asking a friend to come over, calling a relative, ordering pizza over the phone, participating (nonverbally or verbally) in a play, attending a birthday party independently, or coming into the classroom late.

Another helpful step for children or teens experiencing social anxiety is to talk about their feelings with an understanding friend. Individuals with social anxiety often try to mask their discomfort, which can actually make symptoms worse. When socially anxious teens are able to be honest about the anxiety they feel in social situations, they are able to be themselves more, which may reduce their anxiety.

One of the best ways for parents to help their socially anxious child is to create opportunities where both parent and child can be brave together (even if you're just "faking it")! In some cases, especially if you tend to be socially anxious yourself, you may truly feel silly and uncomfortable. For example, try wearing silly hats in public together (or something else that might be noticeably different!). The parent may need to wear the silly hat first, thus bringing attention to themselves. This would probably be an uncomfortable situation for most people! In any case, it is extremely helpful for the parent to note aloud their feelings of anxiety while drawing even more attention to their choice to be brave. You might also discuss aloud how it is hard to be brave at first, but that it gets easier, and that people rarely notice us as much as we believe they do.

Parent *(wearing the silly hat)*: "I'm a little nervous and embarrassed to go out; I'm afraid that people will look at me and they will think I'm ridiculous and will laugh at me! But I know that practicing this will make me braver, and it probably won't be nearly as bad as the alarm system in my brain is telling me it will be!" *(Parent goes out in silly hat)*

Parent: "There are several people looking at me, and that makes me uncomfortable. I'm just going to smile at them and wave, so that they can see I'm not taking myself too seriously. People seem to be enjoying my silly hat – this isn't nearly as bad as I thought it would be! My brain was really sending me alarms that this would be terrible and unbearable, but it's actually kind of fun! I was afraid that everyone would be looking at me, but everyone is so busy living life that they barely even notice me!"

In fact, anytime you are able, create opportunities to model brave behavior and thoughts. At the grocery store you might accidentally drop something (when others are looking) and talk through your thoughts and feelings. "Oh no, how silly, I dropped the butter? That's ok. It's kind of funny. I guess it was slippery! I'll just pick it up and put it in the cart. No problem. I learned from that mistake." By pointing out your mistake, and minimizing your reaction to it, you are helping your child to understand that making mistakes is natural and nothing to be embarrassed about. If mistakes are ok, and I'm not being judged for them, then I may not have to worry so much about my actions.

Additional tips for children with social anxiety include:

- Identify situations that are socially challenging, including joining a conversation, asking a peer to play on the playground, or answering questions in front of the class.
- Learn about and practice relaxation techniques such as visualization, diaphragmatic breathing, and progressive muscle relaxation.
- Identify negative thoughts about social situations and challenge them. For example, "Everyone thinks I look goofy" could be changed to "Nobody has time to think about me – they are worried about what others think of *them*!"
- Pick a challenging situation to practice and develop a plan to tackle the challenge (see the example challenge pathway above).
- Remember to practice good communication and interpersonal skills. For example, good interpersonal skills include listening carefully to what others are saying, making eye contact, nodding or indicating that you are listening to the speaker, and smiling occasionally.
- Create a positive mantra. For example, when facing difficult situations the child could think, "I did it! It was easier than I thought! I am brave enough to do this!"

Understanding and Intervening with Speech/Language Issues

As noted earlier in this manual, many children with SM have co-existing speech/language weaknesses. These can complicate the presentation of SM, since a child who is aware that they don't speak fluently or can't quickly come up with the right words/explanation is more likely to simply stop speaking. Speech therapy is absolutely necessary for children with co-existing SM and speech weaknesses, but obtaining both services can be complicated. Speech therapists may report that they are unable to treat the speech weaknesses if the child doesn't talk to them. On the other hand, the behavioral interventionist may have a hard time understanding the child's speech if the child isn't receiving speech therapy. When the child can speak more as a result of brave work, they may receive negative feedback on their speech (e.g., people request that they repeat things again or others don't understand what they are saying; this could be perceived negatively by the child or increase frustration).

The best-case scenario for these children is a teaming of the speech pathologist and the mental health professional, working in tandem to both increase and improve speech at the same time. The psychologist should work to obtain speech first alone with the child, and then work to transfer or generalize speech to the speech pathologist. When the child is speaking, the speech pathologist might have two goals for treatment – increase speech via brave practice/prompting and reinforcement *and* gentle/slow correction and remediation of speech issues. As speech improves, the psychologist might work to generalize speech to other locations, people, and demands, and they may also assist in creating speaking scenarios where the child is not likely to receive negative feedback.

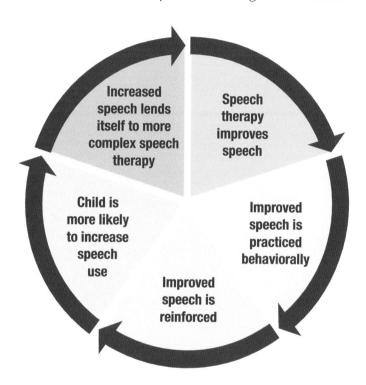

Understanding and Intervening with Defiance/Oppositional Behavior

Researchers believe that children with SM do have slightly higher rates of defiance or oppositionality at home/with parents in comparison to peers (Muris & Ollendick, 2015). This noncompliance can be above and beyond just the avoidance of communication – it is noncompliance with a broad range of parental requests or prompts. As noted before, there could be two main factors influencing the oppositionality:

1) The oppositionality or defiance acts as an avoidance tool against communi-cation or brave work. Children may feel that the only way to reduce anxiety

or discomfort is convincing their parents to rescue them. Therefore, if simply avoiding speech doesn't cause their parents to rescue them, they may engage in defiant or even verbally or physically aggressive behavior to motivate parents to rescue them. Chronic anxiety may also result in a child who appears oppositional even when faced with a seemingly benign request, question, or instruction.

2) The oppositionality and defiance may be unrelated to SM, and instead a stand-alone issue or outcome of behavioral or cognitive rigidity.

Defiance can be an issue when intervening with SM because of the general frustration it causes parents, as well as the resulting difficulty in prompting kids to do brave work. If the child is noncompliant with parental commands or instructions, they are even **more** likely to be noncompliant to instructions that will cause discomfort or anxiety.

What can parents do?

The good news is that parents and caregivers are not the problem– they are the solution!

- ❂ Give appropriate instructions. Instructions or commands should be direct - they should clearly tell the child exactly what you want them to do and when you want them to do it.
    Example – "Tell Dr. Evans where we ate lunch today" instead of "Do you want to tell Dr. Evans where we ate lunch?
    Example – "When we go to the ice cream store today, it's your job to tell the clerk what flavor you want; if you would like I can add in the size and toppings after you tell the flavor" instead of "Maybe you could say what flavor you want at the ice cream store today?"
- ❂ Move slowly through the steps. Don't increase the difficulty level of the challenge faster than your child can tolerate.
- ❂ Incentivize the child with rewards, or have children earn the privileges that they have come to expect (e.g., TV time, access to tablets or phones, internet, etc.) or extra privileges (e.g., extra TV or videogame time, extra dessert, staying up 30 minutes later at night, etc.).
- ❂ If the child gets angry, remember that these are tantrums; that does not mean anxiety does not play a role, but does mean that the behavior shouldn't be encouraged or catered to through "giving in" or giving excessive attention.
- ❂ Ignore the oppositional behavior – most of these behaviors are attempts to avoid unwanted prompts. Calmly restate the prompt after the child calms down. If you *have* to leave and abandon the prompt, either come back after the child calms or let the child know you will be coming back later/ the next day to finish the brave work (and do come back!).

- If you can ignore the behavior, as in the case of tantrums or complaints, do. If you cannot ignore the oppositional behavior, due to aggression (hurting others or destroying things), discipline can be used.
  - State the consequences of the child's behavior with minimal talking and emotion. Do not repeat yourself; you may be invited to argue but you do not have to accept that invitation.
    Example – "We don't hit. When you hit you lose access to your tablet for the rest of the day."
  - Carry out punishment. Discipline should only last 24 hours and should be something the parent can and will enforce.
  - Make sure that the aggressive behavior does not allow the child to be successful in avoiding the brave work. If the child can hit mom and get in trouble, but at the same time mom forgets the brave work prompt, he will likcly be aggressive again because his behavior was successful (e.g., it had the desired outcome of avoiding the brave work).
- For children and parents who need more help, professional consultation and treatment of the oppositionality may be indicated. Parent-Child Interaction Therapy (PCIT) and Parent Management Training (PMT) have been shown to effectively reduce defiance in children with anxiety (Chase & Eyberg, 2008).
- It is worth noting that these children are willing to go to such great lengths to avoid situations that make them anxious because they are trying to cope with feelings that are completely overwhelming for them. If the child tends to be oppositional when they are being prompted to speak (or in other anxiety-provoking situations), they might benefit from a consultation with or treatment by an expert in the field of SM. There truly can be a difference in the outcome when the treatment style is adjusted, considering the level of anxiety the child is experiencing. Experienced therapists can appropriately guide the child and family by knowing when to push and when to adjust the steps along the path.

Understanding and Intervening with Separation Anxiety

Separation anxiety is a fear of separation from caregiver(s) or separation from home. Many children with selective mutism also have separation anxiety; it's unclear if this is because:

- The children have a genetic or temperamental tendency toward anxiety, and therefore they are more likely to present with ANY type of anxiety.
- The children fear that being in certain environments (e.g., school) may require speech or carry social and academic expectations that can be avoided by staying at home.

❖ The children fear being separated from caregivers who are their only means of communication, who may be more likely to rescue, or who are a comfort when they are prompted to speak.

Separation anxiety is best treated with a similar method of "brave work" or graduated exposures. These exposures (what we call "challenge pathways") involve the child separating from the parent for increasing amounts of time, perhaps with rewards attached to brave behavior (staying calm, distracting themselves with play/activities, etc.) during the separations. Additionally, parents are encouraged to remain calm and avoid providing too much comfort/reassurance for the child. Instead, parents should allow the child to practice separating and offer positive but succinct goodbyes (i.e., "I know it makes you feel sad when I leave, but I will be back after school and we will have fun then"). Parents should not become angry or show signs that they are also affected by the separation, as this will inadvertently reinforce the emotional reaction of the child. Additionally, it is recommended that parents do not "sneak" away from the child, because this might promote the feeling that the parent may unexpectedly leave at any moment. Instead, when parents leave, they should exit after providing a quick but warm goodbye, and should not change their plans or stay longer than is recommended (since this may teach the child that crying or becoming upset can keep the parent around longer). Additionally, parents who have children with separation anxiety at school may need to slowly expose their child to increasingly independent separations.

It is important to note that long breaks from school, long illnesses, changes in the home setting, or other stressors can increase separation anxiety and may cause a reset or a brief increase in the level of severity of anxious feelings or behaviors. Parents are encouraged to keep schedules as consistent as possible, avoid bringing the child late to school, and reduce stress at home when possible. In some cases, being one of the first children at school may be helpful. For children with sensory challenges, arriving first diminishes the input a child must take in upon arriving in the classroom – we all know how busy classrooms can get in the morning! They are able to more quickly adjust to the empty classroom and then slowly adjust to each peer as the room becomes fuller. By the way, this trick is great for adults too! It's like "homefield advantage"!

Arriving at School Brave *Example*

About this Game

Help ease your child's transition to school by slowly progressing through levels that will take them from dependence to independence, reducing separation anxiety along the way.

Game Instructions

- Each level represents a milestone in arriving at school independently.
- A check (or sticker) can be earned for each day that the child successfully transitions to school, meeting the expectation for the level at which they are working.
- Treasure Chest Prizes: When a check is earned in a "TC" box, a prize may be chosen from a treasure chest, cither at school or at home.
- When the child reaches a new level, and completes a new challenge, a larger prize may be earned.

Helpful Tips

- Suggested steps are provided, but your child's needs may require a different path.
- Review the game with your child at a time of relative calm. Ask for feedback in determining appropriate steps (if maturity allows) and write steps on the *Preparing for Arriving at School Brave* handout.
- Listen to their concerns.
- Discuss your plan with the teacher and ask for their input. Consider asking the teacher for a special morning job and/or a small token of appreciation they can share with your child for arriving to class brave.
- Avoid starting a new level on a Monday or after a long break from school. A new level will require additional bravery.
- Provide the child with a comfort item to keep in their backpack (if helpful).
- This game is intended as a follow-up, after less intense interventions have failed. If it does not seem to be working for your child, it may not be the right time.
- Try again after some time has passed.

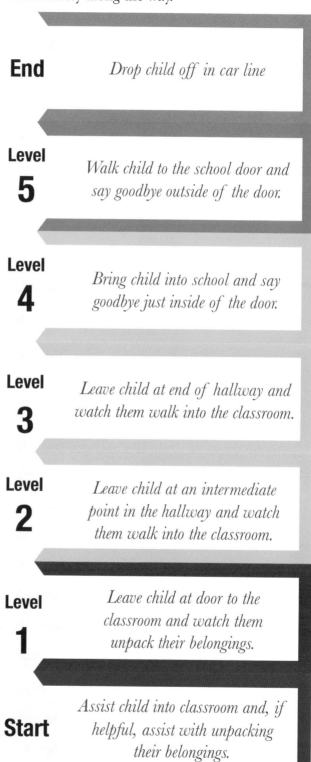

End — *Drop child off in car line*

Level 5 — *Walk child to the school door and say goodbye outside of the door.*

Level 4 — *Bring child into school and say goodbye just inside of the door.*

Level 3 — *Leave child at end of hallway and watch them walk into the classroom.*

Level 2 — *Leave child at an intermediate point in the hallway and watch them walk into the classroom.*

Level 1 — *Leave child at door to the classroom and watch them unpack their belongings.*

Start — *Assist child into classroom and, if helpful, assist with unpacking their belongings.*

Arriving at School Brave Game

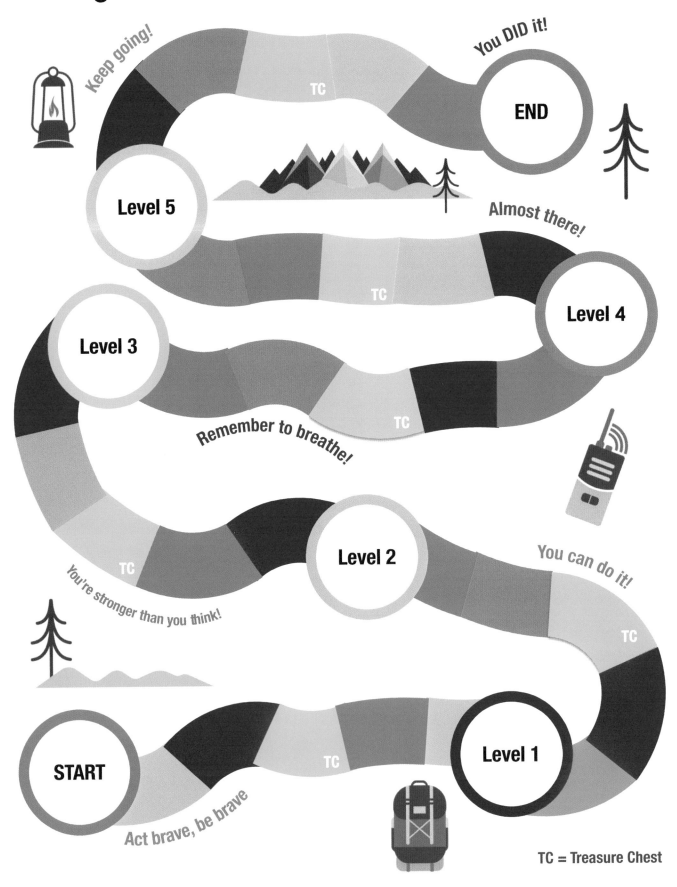

Keep going!

You DID it!

END

Level 5

Almost there!

Level 4

Level 3

Remember to breathe!

You can do it!

You're stronger than you think!

TC

Level 2

TC

START

Act brave, be brave

TC

Level 1

TC = Treasure Chest

Preparing for Arriving at School Brave

Challenge: _____

Instructions:

This worksheet can be used for any challenge requiring small steps toward a larger goal. Assign goals for each level. As much as possible, include your child when determining goals.

Before the challenge

Why does it feel hard?

How can we make it feel easier?

How will we feel when we complete this challenge?

After the challenge

We did it! What was the hardest part?

What did we learn?

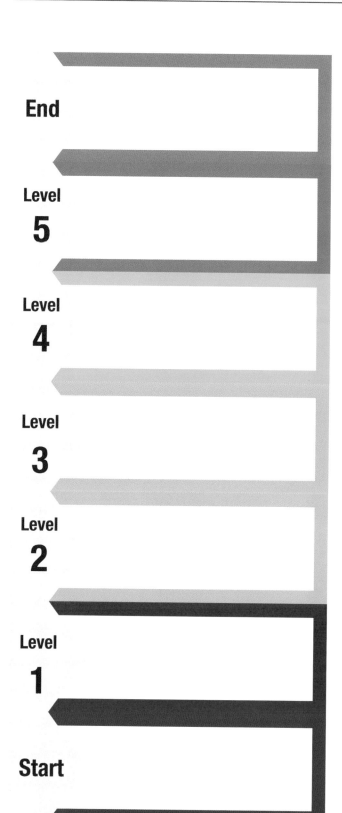

End

Level
5

Level
4

Level
3

Level
2

Level
1

Start

Autism spectrum disorder (ASD) is a collection of symptoms associated with difficulty in social relatedness and social understanding, among other symptoms. Technically, SM and autism are not intended to be diagnosed together (per the DSM-5, the diagnostic manual for mental health professionals). As SM may look very similar to ASD to those who are new to the condition (due to apparent differences in communication, eye contact, and socialization), it is probably important that the DSM-5 does highlight the differences between the two disorders in order to limit misdiagnoses. Nevertheless, most professionals agree that SM and ASD can and do co-exist for some children

A child with both SM and autism might have anxiety surrounding speaking, along with communication weaknesses, immature social skills, a lack of understanding of social expectations and social rules, and possibly a disinterest in social interactions. A child with only SM may demonstrate some of these same symptoms when anxious, but relates and socializes in a typical manner when in comfortable situations.

The gold-standard treatment for autism is Applied Behavioral Analysis (ABA), where the clinician breaks down the behavioral goals into small steps and reinforces the child when they successfully practice those social steps (very similar to the behavioral intervention for selective mutism!). When working with a young child with both SM and autistic qualities, the weaknesses inherit to autism will likely need to be treated first or at the same time as SM through ABA.

If the treatment focus is on intervening with selective mutism, and a child presents with some characteristics of autism, there are a few differences in expectations and intervention. More visual reminders are used, explanations and prompts given are very concrete, and communication partners are careful to prompt for factual responses as opposed to questions about preferences, feelings, or experiences. For example, the questions asked of a child with both SM and autism might focus on identifying items in the environment or providing factual information rather than ambiguous or personal questions (which may be harder for the child with autism). Instead of asking how his day was, what he feels about something, or his opinions about the recent field trip, the teacher might ask him what insects he saw or who he sat with on the bus. Furthermore, treatment or intervention for a child with both SM and ASD may need to move more slowly and may take longer.

Finally, parents and professionals will need to keep in mind that unlike children with only an SM diagnosis, social interactions may not be internally motivating for children with co-existing autism. Generally, social interactions are motivating and feel good even for children with SM, especially as anxiety diminishes through brave practice. However, we cannot assume that children with co-occurring selective mutism and autism will continue attempting social interactions after doing their brave work just because it feels good to talk, have friends, and relate verbally to people. They may need more tangible reinforcements (rewards) for brave work (since the internal motivation may not be there) and more time and effort may be necessary to help them understand or to frequently remind them of the reasons that talking is useful (e.g., it helps us get the things that we want, it keeps us safe and out of trouble, etc.).

Despite the best efforts of parents, some of these issues may require more intervention. If your child continues to be impacted by separation anxiety, speech issues, autism characteristics, or defiance, reach out to a mental health expert for support and guidance.

A Final Note...

There is no interventionist quite like a parent. We are our child's best advocate, their friend, their coach, their helper, and their biggest fan. The work that you do with your child may be a challenge, but it could also be their best success.

"Challenges are what makes life more interesting
and overcoming them is what makes life meaningful."
–Joshua J. Marine

FREQUENTLY ASKED QUESTIONS ABOUT SELECTIVE MUTISM

Question: How do I explain SM to family/friends or the general public?
Answer: Spreading awareness about selective mutism is incredibly important.

- ☑ It will increase empathy for your child's anxiety
- ☑ It will increase the likelihood that adults and peers are willing to help intervene
- ☑ It may help others identify children with SM who would have otherwise just been considered shy or stubborn

Providing information to family, friends, schools, extracurricular coaches, and pediatricians is vital, but is best done in small doses. Parents can give a short explanation outlining SM as an anxiety disorder that makes it very difficult for the child to speak in public and social situations, and provide tips such as:

- ☑ Ask my child forced-choice questions (not yes/no questions but questions where they choose from two different answers)
- ☑ Wait a few moments for them to answer, even if it is uncomfortable
- ☑ Don't be afraid to speak to them directly, or to comment or acknowledge what you hear them saying to me
- ☑ Don't try to force or coerce them to talk, but instead spend one-on-one time with them and build a positive relationship with them

Question: How do I correct peers and siblings who rescue?
Answer: Many siblings or peers are well-meaning rescuers, and rescue for two reasons - to help the child feel better and because of a lack of understanding about the best role in helping the child become stronger. The first step is to educate other children about SM, why it happens, and what

friends or siblings can do to support your child. A great explanation is found in the book <u>Charli's Choices</u>, by Marian B. Moldan. The book explains SM in a child-friendly format and discusses great techniques for children to utilize, including asking forced-choice questions, waiting for an answer, and not answering for the child with SM (since this hinders them from becoming brave). For a young child in preschool, this book might be read to the whole class without the child present. It is important that peers understand that the child does talk at home, is working hard to be brave, and will speak at school when they are ready. Then, a class discussion could occur about how to be a good friend even though the child with SM does not speak yet. Peers can approach the child and ask them to play, understand that just because they don't speak to you doesn't mean they don't like you, and remember not to overreact when they do speak. Parents might also let their child know that the class is discussing ways to be a good friend, as well as helping classmates understand their child better.

For older children (who may be very embarrassed to hear that a discussion about them occurred in class), parents and school personnel may want to pull individual children aside and discuss these topics.

Alternatively, children may wish to write a letter to their class or record a video at home, explaining both their interests and unique challenges and listing ways friends can be helpful.

Question: How should I plan for the upcoming school year?

Answer: Consideration of the next school year should always start by April of the current year. The school team and parents should carefully consider how to transition the child successfully to the next year without losing any momentum, and which teacher may be a good match for the child. It is recommended that the child spend some time with the new teacher prior to the start of the school year (perhaps by being a "helper" in setting up and organizing the classroom). This allows for the child to establish or re-establish speech with the teacher and get comfortable in the new classroom.

Parents should also request a school meeting at the start of every school year to educate the new staff on SM, update gains acquired over the summer, and update goals and interventions to be used in the new year. This meeting can also include discussions about upcoming challenges embedded in the school year (e.g., 4th graders have to present at the "Historical Wax Museum" – how will the child with SM tackle this particular challenge, and how can the team plan and prepare for it?).

Question: How do I respond when people call my child "shy"?

Answer: Generally, it is recommended that parents and others avoid using or identifying with the term "shy," since it suggests that the child is temperamentally inhibited and will always be this way. Many children will also label themselves "shy" to avoid brave tasks (e.g., "I can't do that…I'm shy, remember?"). There will always be strangers in public who refer to the child as "shy," and parents may wish to ignore this and move on, having private discussions with the child that they are NOT shy but instead are feeling anxious in certain situations because of an overactive brain alarm ("…and we are working hard to correct that alarm or teach you how to ignore it so everyone can see what a cool kid you are!"). Alternatively, parents may wish to be more direct, simply responding, "Oh, Brayden is actually very talkative when he is comfortable, and he is working very hard to be brave in public too!"

Question: Is this just being stubborn?

Answer: There is no evidence to suggest that children with SM are more stubborn than typically-developing children, or that they receive any notable social or tangible benefit from not speaking (as you would expect if they are being stubborn). Instead, many children with SM miss out on enjoyable activities and they often voice their desire to speak… but the words just get stuck. For many children with SM, not being able to speak may be a frustrating and confidence-killing situation.

There are some strong-willed children who also have SM. For these children, stubbornness isn't the primary cause of a lack of speech but it might interfere with their willingness to talk. Playful, encouraging, covert intervention can still work very well to increase speech. Instead of being very overt in the steps that the child is taking toward brave work, parents can simply engage the child in situations and then prompt for the response they are seeking. When the child responds, the parent gives a matter-of-fact acknowledgement or makes no mention of the speech and moves on (as opposed to providing a lot of attention or reinforcement for speech). For some children, any acknowledgment or praise for speaking is not well tolerated in the beginning. However, as the child's confidence builds so will their threshold for praise. Consider peppering in casual verbal praise to build tolerance for accepting praise.

It is important that parents help others to understand that SM is not defiance or stubbornness. When adults or peers believe that the child is purposefully withholding speech, they may react with either anger and coercion toward the child ("He can talk; we will just make sure he doesn't get to eat his lunch or go to recess until he talks!") or with annoyance and social dismissal ("She just doesn't like me - if she liked me, she would talk to me"). Forcing, coercing, or resorting to yelling or punishment to enforce speech is not a successful long-term intervention tool for children with SM. Being fun and engaging, building a relationship with the child, and prompting for the child to face their fears at a reasonable pace works!

Question: What should I do about siblings who present with a hesitancy to speak?

Answer: At times, younger siblings will model the behavior of an older sibling with SM. Some older siblings will even teach or tell their younger siblings not to talk! If modeling appears to be the primary reason for a lack of speech from siblings, parents can purposefully reinforce speaking as well as hold desirable activities and items contingent on speech (e.g., "I need to know what kind of sandwich you want me to make – do you want a turkey sandwich with cheese or a PB&J?").

If it appears that the sibling truly does have symptoms associated with SM (e.g., the child has difficulty speaking even when not accompanied by the older sibling, simple prompts and rewards for speech don't work, or other anxiety symptoms are present), then the sibling may also have selective mutism. Since SM is an anxiety disorder, and anxiety disorders have a biological, genetic, and environmental (learning) component, siblings are at a higher likelihood for also developing the disorder (this is particularly true of twins). Parents are recommended to have the sibling evaluated for SM and consider intervention if it appears to be necessary. The good news is that knowledgeable parents will be able to use brave work with both siblings (each at their own levels of ability) and may even be able to create some healthy competition surrounding communication (which might increase speech in both siblings!).

Question: What about adolescents with SM? How are treatment and outcomes different?

Answer: Much less is known about adolescents and adults with SM, due to low frequency of occurrence and a lack of good research on this age group. Carl Sutton and Cheryl Forrester authored an interesting book on the experiences of adults with SM (Selective Mutism In Our Own Words: Experiences in Childhood and Adulthood); however, these experiences do not teach us exactly how to modify our treatment or expectations for teens and adults with SM. We do know that older children, adolescents, and adults are generally more challenging to treat and will likely need a longer intervention. This may occur because they have become accustomed to not speaking, and it is very hard to change a habit. They have often found ways of communicating or getting their needs met nonverbally, and this is much easier than the hard work it would take to speak. Additionally, they have become known as someone who doesn't talk, and speaking will likely garner a huge reaction from people!

When intervening with adolescents and young adults, there are a few key differences:

- The adolescent will likely need medication in addition to behavioral treatment, as many adolescents and young adults have more severe symptoms and more co-occurring disorders, such as depression, social anxiety, agoraphobia (the fear of places or situations which might leave the individual feeling trapped, panicked, or embarrassed), etc.

- Intervention will likely take longer and may include treating social anxiety and learning independent living skills in addition to working on the fear of speaking.

- A cognitive behavioral approach (as opposed to the generally behavioral approach that this book takes) may be helpful in working with teens and adults with SM. Cognitive behavioral therapy (CBT) utilizes exposures (like brave work in this book), but also asks the individual to think about their perceptions or thoughts and how these thoughts may increase anxiety. For instance, a teen may think, "If I talk in class, everyone will look at me and laugh" and this may inhibit them from speaking. CBT encourages "testing" those thoughts through brave practices, as well as working to correct or replace unhelpful thoughts with more helpful, balanced ones.

- The adolescent will need to be engaged in the treatment and motivated to make change. While parents of young kids can bring their children into the clinic without the child's full agreement or desire to come, bringing a teen against their will is markedly more difficult! Much of the discussion on motivation and change has to occur through the parent at first. The parent can begin to talk to the teen about the benefits and costs of not speaking, how they imagine their future if they continue to be unable to speak, when they think they would like to make a change, and how they think that change will occur.

School interventions for adolescents/young adults also presents a challenge. By high school or college, direct intervention in the school is more minimal while expectations for independence, self-advocacy, and verbal participation in the classroom increase dramatically. Parents often need to advocate for services, including a "keyworker" who assists in developing and carrying out the intervention plan at school. It is of utmost importance that the adolescent has a positive relationship with the keyworker, and feels comfortable with them, so that they have at least one adult in the school with whom they can interact successfully. Using a stimulus fading or shaping procedure may be necessary to elicit speech, so parents should request one-on-one meetings with the keyworker and student or with the student and main teachers (again, this is more difficult to obtain in middle or high school settings, as well as in college, so advocating will be necessary).

In addition to assigning a keyworker, allowing the student alternative ways of presenting and earning participation points until the student can use their voice is helpful.

Question: **What should I do if my child or adolescent will not participate in therapy?**
Answer: This can happen, especially with adolescents. The first-line intervention when kids cannot or will not be active participants in the intervention is to incentivize them to do so, either through privilege-earning or rewards. We must all "work" for the benefits we get in life, and it is okay for parents to insist that the benefits that kids receive (e.g., cell phones, internet access, car access, TV) must be earned by the "work" of attending and participating in therapy. However, there are still children/adolescents who do not comply despite these contingencies, and parents frequently feel helpless. Dr. Eli Leibowitz at Yale University has developed the SPACE program, a parent-training program for childhood anxiety disorders. This intervention has demonstrated good outcomes when involving parents in the treatment even when the child is reluctant to make changes. This parent-based intervention teaches parents how to decrease accommodation for the child's anxiety and positively prompt them to make changes (Leibowitz, Omer, Hermes, & Scahill, 2003). There is still hope for making positive changes, even if your child isn't ready to actively participate in brave work.

REFERENCES

Bartarian, J. A., Sanchez, J. M., Magen, J., Siroky, A. K., Mash, B. L., & Carlson, J. S. (2018). An Examination of Fluoxetine for the Treatment of Selective Mutism Using a Nonconcurrent Multiple-Baseline Single-Case Design Across 5 Cases. *Journal of Psychiatric Practice*, 2-14.

Bergman, R. L., Gonzalez, A., Piacentini, J., & Keller, M. L. (2013). Integrated Behavior Therapy for Selective Mutism: A randomized controlled pilot study. *Behaviour research and therapy*, 680-689.

Bergman, R.L. Treatment for children with selective mutism: An integrative behavioral approach. New York, New York. Oxford University Press.

Black, B. &. (1994). Treatment of elective mutism with fluoxetine: A double-blind, placebo controlled study. *Journal of American Academy of Child and Adolescent Psychiatry*, 1000-1006.

Carpenter, A. P. (2014, Dec.). Extending Parent–Child Interaction Therapy for Early Childhood Internalizing Problems: New Advances for an Overlooked Population. *Clinical Child and Family Psychological Review*, 340-356.

Chase, R. E. & Eyberg, S.M. (2008). Clinical presentation and treatment outcome for children with comorbid externalizing and internalizing symptoms. *Journal of Anxiety Disorders*, 273-282.

Compton, S. N., Albano, A. M., Piacentini, J., Birmaher, B., Sherill, J., Ginsberg, G., . . . March, J. (2010). Child/Adolescent Anxiety Multimodal Study (CAMS): rationale, design, and methods. *Child and Adolescent Psychiatry and Mental Health*.

Dummit, E. K. (1996). Fluoxetine treatment of children with selective mutism: An open trial. *Journal of the American Academy of Child and Adolescent Psychiatry*, 615-621.

Dummit, E. S., Klein, R. G., Tancer, N. K., Asche, B., Martin, J., & Fairbanks. (1997). Systematic assessment of 50 children with selective mutism. *Journal of the American Academy of Child and Adolescent Psychiatry*, 653–660.

Food and Drug Administration . (2016, April 13). *Antidepressant Use in Children, Adolescents, and Adults*. Retrieved from US Dept of Health and Human Services: https://www.fda.gov/Drugs/DrugSafety/InformationbyDrugClass/ucm096273.htm

Grice, K. (2002). Eligibility under IDEA for other health impaired children. *School Law Bulletin*, 8-12.

Head Start. (2006). *Policy and Regulations for Eligibility Criteria: Speech and Language Impairments.* Retrieved December 20, 2013, from Head Start: http://eclkc.ohs.acf.hhs.gov/hslc/standards/Head%20Start%20Requirements/1308/1308.9%20%20Eligibility%20criteria_%20Speech%20or%20language%20impairments..htm

Johnson, M., & Wintgens, A. (2017). *The Selective Mutism Resource Manual* (2nd ed.). London: Routledge.

Kearney, C. &. (2006). Functional analysis and treatment of selective mutism in children. *Jouranl of Speech-Language Pathology and Applied Behavioral Analysis*, 141-148.

Kristensen, H. (2001). Multiple informants' report of emotional and behavioural problems in a nation-wide sample of selective mute children and controls,. *European Child and Adolescent Psychiatry*, 135–142.

Kurtz, S. K. (2013). Intensive treatment of selective mutism. *Presented at the Selective Mutism Group Annual Conference.* Berkeley, CA.

Kurtz (2015). Verbal-Directed Interaction (VDI) Skills. *Kurtz Psychology Consulting PC.*

Leibowitz, E. O. (2003). Parent training for childhood anxiety disorders: The SPACE program. *Cognitive and Behavioral Practice.*

Mayo Clinic Staff (2017). Relaxation Techniques: Try These Steps to Reduce Stress. Retrieved from https://www.mayoclinic.org/healthy-lifestyle/stress-management/in-depth/relaxation-technique/art-20045368

McNeil, C. H.-K. (2010). *Parent-Child Interaction Therapy (Issues in Clinical Child Psychology).* Springer.

Miller, A. (2017, March 28). (A. Kotrba, Interviewer)

Mulligan, C., & Shipon-Blum, E. (2015). (2015). Selective Mutism: Identification of Subtypes and Implications for Treatment. *Journal of Education and Human Development.*

Muris, P., Gadet, B., Moulaert, V., & Merckelbach, H. (1998). Correlations between two multidimensional anxiety scales for children. *Perceptual and Motor Skills, 87*(1), 269-270. doi:10.2466/pms.1998.87.1.269

Muris, P. O. & Ollendick, T.H. (2015). Children who are anxious in silence: A review on Selective Mutism, the new anxiety disorder in DSM-5. *Clin Child Fam Psychol Rev*, 151-169.

Oerbeck, B., Overgaard, K., Stein, M., Pripp, A., & Kristensen, H. (2018). Treatment of Selective Mutism: A 5 year follow up study. *European Jouranl of Child and Adolescent Psychiatry*.

Oerbeck, B., Stein, M., Wentzel-Larsen, T., Langsrud, O., & Kristensen, H. (2013). A randomized controlled trial of a home and school-based intervention for selective mutism - defocused communicaiton and behavioural techniques. *Child and Adolescent Mental Health*.

Pionek-Stone, B., Kratochwill, T. R., Sladezcek, I., & Serlin, R. C. (2002). Treatment of selective mutism: A best-evidence synthesis. *School Psychology Quarterly*, 168.

Reynolds, C.R., & Kamphaus, R.W. (2015). Behavior Assessment System for Children (3rd edition). Circle Pines, MN: American Guidance Service.

Services, K. C. (2017, April 21). *VDI Updated 10/15/15*. Retrieved from Selective Mutism Learning University: http://selectivemutismlearning.org/wp-content/uploads/2015/10/VDI-UPDATED-10-15-15.pdf

Vecchio, J., & Kearney, C. (2009). Treating youths with selective mutism with an alternating design of exposure-based practice and contingency management. *Behavior Therapy*, 380-392.

Wright, P. & Wright, P. (2007). *Wrightslaw : Special Education Law*. Hartfield, Va: Harbor House Law Press.

Printed in Great Britain
by Amazon